Two

GOD AND MAN

GOD AND MAN

METROPOLITAN ANTHONY
OF SOUROZH

Darton, Longman and Todd
London

St Vladimir's Seminary Press
Crestwood, New York 10707
1983

First published in 1978 by
Darton, Longman and Todd Ltd
89 Lillie Road, London SW6 1UD

Fourth impression 1979

This edition published 1983
together with
St Vladimir's Seminary Press
575 Scarsdale Road
Crestwood, New York 10707

ISBN 0 232 51607 3 (DLT)
ISBN 0-88141-024-1 (SVS Press)

Printed and bound in Great Britain by
Anchor Brendon Ltd
Tiptree, Essex

CONTENTS

1. The Atheist and the Archbishop   7

2. Doubt and the Christian Life   31

3. Man and God   49

4. Holiness and Prayer   73

5. John the Baptist   121

CHAPTER ONE

THE ATHEIST AND THE ARCHBISHOP[1]

Marghanita Laski and Archbishop Anthony Bloom

I

Laski: You believe in God, and you think this is good and right. I don't believe in God, and I think it's good and right. Now we're neither of us frivolous people, we're serious, we've reached our decision as carefully as we can. There's a lot of people like me, there's a lot of people, probably a lot more people, like you. How do you explain this basic, one could say this *fundamental* difference?

Bloom: I really don't know how to explain it but it seems to me that the word 'belief' is misleading. It gives an impression of something optional, which is within our powers to choose or not. What I feel very strongly about it, is that I believe because I know that God exists, and I'm puzzled how you manage not to know.

Laski: This brings me to the next thing I wanted to ask you, which is about faith. I know that faith is a major Christian virtue but to me it's nearer a vice and I cannot see why you need it. When you say 'I know that God exists' and many people do say this for one reason or another because they've experienced God or because they see God in the shape of the universe. But if you know, you don't need faith. And if you don't know, to me as an unbeliever, it's almost throwing away the most important

---

[1] Transcript of televised interviews, transmitted 5th and 12th July, 1970; with grateful acknowledgement to the BBC.

thing about a human being, to substitute faith for not knowing. To me, the right thing when you don't know is to wait on knowledge or to say 'I don't know'. If you know that God exists, why should faith be considered a virtue?

Bloom: I think it's a question of the definition of faith. I remember having read in a rather facetious theological book a definition of faith as the ability which grown-ups possess to assert that things are true when they know that they are not true.

Laski: That's rather nice . . . .

Bloom: If that is faith, I'm afraid I don't possess it. I think faith is best defined in the words of the Epistle to the Hebrews, when the writer says 'Faith is certainty about things invisible.' It is certainty, that is the operative word, and things which are invisible are not simply things imagined. Speaking for instance of myself and a number of other people, I'm sure we began with an experience that was totally convincing. Now at a certain moment this experience faded away, as does every experience of beauty, of love, of joy, of pain. There is a moment when it is no longer actual, but the certainty of it has remained. And this is the moment when faith comes into it. But faith doesn't mean credulity; it means that the certainty remains about something which is not our actual present experience of things.

Laski: If you use the word faith, surely it must imply that you have faith in the face of possible doubt? But if you have certainty, then there's no room for doubt, and so I'm sorry, I can't see any need for faith—isn't certainty enough?

Bloom: You are in the same position as I in a way. You have a certainty, concerning the non-existence of God, which in a way is an act of faith, because you have as little evidence you can produce outwardly as I have to produce outwardly.

Laski: Wouldn't you say there was a fundamental difference in way of thinking about, or way of approaching problems of the invisible, that there could be a temperamental preference for having certainty about the invisible, and for reserving judgment about the invisible?

Bloom: I'm not sure, I think my attitude to things is very much determined by the kind of education I have had. I was trained to be a scientist and I treat things as experimental science—perhaps wrongly, perhaps rightly. But as far as faith is concerned, for instance, I started with something which was an experience which seemed to be convincing, that God does exist. Doubt comes into it not as questioning this fundamental experience but as questioning my intellectual workings out of it. And in that respect the doubt of the believer should be as creative, as daring, as joyful, almost as systematic as the doubt of a scientist who, having discovered facts that have convinced him up to a point of something, will begin to find the flaw in his reasoning, the error in his system, or new facts that will invalidate his model of the universe.

Laski: But his moment of discovering, as it seems to him, a new pattern in the universe, is equally convincing whether his examination of the pattern shows it to be true or false. The scientist will no doubt value the feeling that comes with the new discovery, but he wouldn't regard that feeling as validating, as you say; he would afterwards make tests and so on. But you don't, do you, admit an experience of feeling as if God exists which doesn't necessarily say whether God exists or not?

Bloom: I don't think it's wholly a question of feeling. I don't think for instance that feeling can be simply unreasonable or completely absurd, and yet kept against every other evidence. But I would say for instance if you transfer, for a moment, from faith in God to other fields—music, say—from the point of view of a scientist, music can be put in drawing, in line, in mathematical formula. When you've got them all it does not give you a clue as to whether this is a beautiful piece of music or whether it is just discordant noise. There is a moment when you listen and you say this is music and not simply noise.

Laski: Certainly, although one of the things I most want to know about is why good music, good poetry, good art, has the effect on us it does, and I always assume that experiences of God include such a patterning. I as an atheist would never want to doubt the profound knowledge that the Churches, synagogues, mosques, have acquired over the centuries, into human nature, into human thought, into human physical responses. Now you've written greatly about interior prayer and even before I read your book I was very much interested in this because it seemed to me clearly that it worked. That is to say, people who attempted contemplative prayer received benefit from it. And this I have tried, I have tried it a great deal recently, because I've just had a very bad slipped disc, and I don't like painkillers. And it seemed to me that to try contemplative prayer, as St Gregory describes it, meditating on the Lord's Prayer for instance, might help my pain. And indeed it did. So I assume that here the Church has discovered a mental technique which is therapeutic, which is beneficial. But it seems to me that in the case of this experience of prayer, as in other experiences called religious, the Church has, so to speak, pre-empted them, said 'These are our experiences, these lead to God.' I'm not pretending my attempts compare with anything that a trained religious could do, but are you not holding to yourselves and giving explanations which are unacceptable to atheists of various techniques and modes of living that could help all humanity, perhaps even in this time of recourse to drugs —could help humanity with greater need than ever before?

Bloom: As far as techniques and methods are concerned, I quite agree that you are right, and I could give you an example in your favour as it were, about a group of drug addicts who by chance read 'The Cloud of Unknowing' and addressed themselves to a priest, not to me, to say: 'We have discovered that this is exactly what we are looking for and it would be a much cheaper thing for us to get it that way than through the drugs we are using—'

Laski: —And much healthier.

Bloom: Much healthier. And we have experience now of a number of drug addicts for instance who discover through meditation what they were looking for through drugs, and move away from drugs into another world. As far as technique is concerned I think it is completely true, because techniques are founded on our common humanity. Whatever the object you pursue, your thinking is your human thinking, your emotions and feelings are your human emotions and so forth. What the believer would say is that for some reason, the same kind of reason that makes you recognise beauty in music, in nature, in art and so on, he would say: 'This experience which I had is neither my emotions nor my wishful thinking, nor my physical condition at that moment; it was a meeting with something different, profoundly other than myself, and which I cannot trace back even with decent knowledge of sociology, or psychology, or biology, to anything which is me, and within me.'

Laski: This is the fundamental difference between us, isn't it? Whether this feeling that we have encountered is something other than oneself, is a self-induced feeling or is an other-induced feeling, an other-derived feeling. Is this not what separates us most?

Bloom: Yes. A believer would say: 'I objectively know that he exists, which means I have knowledge acquired and not manufactured.' But doesn't it apply in the same way to things like irrational experiences in common life? Like love, like the sense of beauty, in art, music and so on?

Laski: I would guess that the sense of beauty is irrational only for the present until explained. I always think of the philosopher Hume, who two hundred years ago said we know that bread does us good but we shall never know why and of course now we do know why. And I think we shall, perhaps in the not very distant future, come to learn what kind of patterning it is that affects us and that we call beautiful.

Bloom: That may well be, but why don't you think that we may by the same process come to a point when by the study, say, of brainwaves and that kind of thing, we will be able to discover that at such a moment something has intruded or come into our experience which is not intrinsic to our physical body. Logically, it's as credible as the other one.

Laski: This is what I would most like to know and of course if the experiment worked your way, there would be no alternative to being a believer. I simply suspect it would work my way. But Archbishop, supposing I had, as any of us unbelievers might have, a sudden experience of the kind you describe as certainty that God existed. Supposing that it didn't take place in any religious context. Let's say like St Ignatius Loyola, I was sitting by a river. Now I know I was brought up a Jew, but I've lived in England, which is as they say the country of a hundred religions and one sauce, why should anything follow from this? I can understand that it would be sensible to join a religion for fear of the kind of arrogant madness that falls upon people who think that they have a direct personal line to God, but from this experience of God, what should lead me to suppose I've encountered a Christian, a Jewish, a Moslem God? That he would want me to be a Methodist or a Russian Orthodox or a Church of England? What should make one take a step further than having this experience and saying: 'Fine, I now have the certainty that God exists?'

Bloom: It would proceed in different steps—if you had, and I'm certain one can have an experience of God outside any context, of previous religiosity or religious background, then you will probably discover that if God does exist it has immediate implications as to your situation with regard to men in general. . . .

Laski: Please explain because this is what I want to understand.

Bloom: Readily. My experience in childhood was that life was violent, brutal, heartless, that men were to one another adversaries and causes of suffering, that there were on the whole just a few, the closest around you, who belonged together, and who were no danger to you. And my situation when I was a young teenager, was that all these people were dangers. One had to fight, to overcome in order to survive, and eventually to hit back as hard as one could in order to win the day.

Laski: This was truly your situation, I believe, wasn't it?

Bloom: That was the experience I had, in a slum school, and in the early years of revolution and so on—not in Russia but abroad. Now, when I discovered God and I discovered Him in connection with the Gospel, the first thing that struck me is that here was a God for whom everyone was meaningful, who was not segregating people, who was not the God of the good versus the bad, the God of the believer versus the unbeliever, the God of one type versus another. That everyone existed for him as a completely meaningful and valuable person. And if I had discovered that God, then that was the attitude I had to discover with regard to all my surroundings. And you know, I felt with amazement that the fact that I had discovered that God was such, and that that was his relatedness to everyone else, upturned me completely. I looked around and I no longer saw the detestable hateful creatures, but people who were in relationship with Him, and with whom I could come into a new relationship, if I believed about them what God believes about them.

Laski: But it is a fact that non-believers can have this experience of respectful love, charitable love, to all creatures, without the need for God. I'm not a good Socialist, but I think that people who are really good Socialists, in the basic sense, not the political sense of the word, have this feeling. It's not necessary to have God to have the sense of the worth of each human being.

Bloom: No, I don't mean to say that it is necessary. I would say it is not necessary to know that God exists to be a human being, and not below the mark as I was quite definitely. Neither is it necessary I would say, to know that God exists for Him to exist in fact. To me the problem of God is this. He is not something I need to have a world outlook. I don't need God to fill gaps in my world outlook. I have discovered that he exists and I can't help it, exactly in the same way as I have discovered facts in science. He is a fact for me, and that's why He has significance and plays a role in a way exactly in the same sense in which having discovered that a person exists, life becomes different from the moment before you had become aware of the person.

Laski: Could I ask you to be a bit concrete about this? For instance this is rather a debating point I'm going to make, but I thing it's a valid one. For the past five hundred years, since science escaped from the bounds of the Church, it's leapt ahead, so that it's a commonplace now to say that our technological, our scientific knowledge is beyond our moral capacity. The Church, on the other hand, has had two thousand years to develop our moral capacity, if this is one of its functions. But you have said that one can come to this awareness of the real individual—what's the Christian word I want?—for the existence, the respectful existence of every human being. And this entails, I think, a kind of behaviour to human beings which makes a link between belief in God and morals. Is there a necessary link between belief in God and morals? What is it? And since the Church doesn't seem in two thousand years to have made us good—in fact I would claim that it's secular thought that has done most to improve us over the past two hundred years—can the Church be said to have fulfilled this function? In other words, how do morals follow from belief in God? Why has the Church failed to make us moral beings?

Bloom: I think quite certainly morals should follow our belief in God because if we see the world structured around a certain number of great principles, it should make a difference to our behaviour. . .

Laski: What are the great principles?

Bloom: Love, let us say. . . love, justice.

Laski: Because you feel love when you encounter God? Because God seems to be a creature of love and justice?—I mean where do these virtues come into the encounter with God?

Bloom: Let me limit myself to the Gospel which will be easier than to try to embrace a wider field. The whole teaching of the Gospel is really a teaching about loving. Now the fact that we fall short of it condemns us, but doesn't make its declaration less true. I'm quite prepared to say that individually and collectively we have fallen very short of that ideal. Now what I'm more doubtful about, is what you said about secular thought because my impression is that west European secular thought at least, or the secular thought developed from west European culture is impregnated with the Gospel, for instance the notion of the value of the person is something which the Gospel has introduced into ancient society which simply didn't possess it. And there are so many things which now have become common ground, universally accepted, which were novelties in their time and which now work in society as leaven works in dough.

Laski: I would agree with you completely about this. I'm only saying that over the past two hundred years, at least since the middle of the eighteenth century, these principles which do seem to me to be the glory of western civilisation, have passed effectively into the hands of the seculars and from the hands of the religious, that insofar as there has been a moral leap forward over this period, and I think there has been one, it's not I think, the Churches, the synagogues, that we have to thank for it.

Bloom: There are two things that strike me—the one is that the believers have had and still have a most unfortunate tendency to escape the difficulties and the problems of life into 'worship' in inverted commas.

Laski: Yes, I'm glad you brought that up.

Bloom: That quite certainly. It's much easier to retire to one's room and say: 'Oh God, give bread to the hungry,' than to do something about it. I have just been in America and someone was making discourse about his readiness to give his life for the hungry and the needy, and I asked him why he was a chain smoker and didn't give simply a packet of cigarettes for it.

Laski: And I can throw another example at you. All of us who have children and meet a lot of young people . . . . meet the people who ask for more love in the world but find it impossible to give it to the older generation.

Bloom: Yes, that's true too. So that is quite definite. We have been escaping into a world of irresponsible prayer, instead of realising that if I say to God, 'Here is a need. Help,' I must be prepared to hear God answer within me, without waiting for a revelation. 'You have seen that—well go and do it.' So that is a way in which we have failed, and which is one of the reasons why we have gone wrong.

Laski: Could I suggest that another reason why I think you and the secular do-gooders also have failed is because of a rejection of the world not just as you say, going into one's room and failing to do the good that lies to hand, but a feeling that the world and particularly the urban world of today, is a hell— a Satanic mill, a place to be avoided. There's no gaiety in religion, for instance, there's no enjoyment of a jolly life. The pleasures that we normally take in society, even if you like the pleasures of amassing possessions, of sitting in our little castles with our refrigerators round us and our children playing at our feet—these to me are healthful pleasures. But I think that serious people, serious religious people, serious non-religious people, have always regarded these things that we genuinely enjoy as human animals, as clogs in the way of the good life.

Bloom: I think they are right up to a point. I think it takes a great deal of mastery of self not to forget what is deepest in oneself to the profit of what is more superficial. It's easier to be superficial than deep, it's easier to be on that level rather than face things that may be tragic. You see the difficulty is that we have made it into a false moral attitude, into an attitude that if you are a Christian you must be stern, almost sinister, never laugh—

Laski: —Or very, very simple, so simple and innocent that the realities of life seem irrelevant to you.

Bloom: Yes. But if you are really aware of things, of how tragic life is, then there is restraint in your enjoyment. Joy is another thing. One can possess a great sense of inner joy and elation, but enjoying the outer aspects of life with the awareness of so many people suffering and so on, is something which I find difficult. When I was a professional man, we made a decision with my mother never to live beyond the minimum which we need for shelter and food because we thought and I still think, that whatever you spend above that, it is stolen from someone else who needs it while you don't need it. That doesn't make you sinister, it gives you a sense of joy in sharing, and in giving and receiving. But I do feel that as long as there is one person who is hungry, excess of happiness—excess of amenities—is a theft. . .

Laski: And yet each one person is so vulnerable, so prone to tragedy, so likely to fall into danger that when I see people, for instance on a beach, with excessive possessions and enjoying themselves excessively, here I think, is gaiety, a little happiness stored, a moment of gaiety that is not wrong.

Bloom: I wouldn't say it is wrong. I think it could be deeper and it could be more permanent. One of the problems of the modern person is that we have so much that we no longer enjoy little things. Say, in the years when life was extremely hard, in my experience, the slightest joy was a miracle. Now, my level of miracle has come up; it takes more for me to find that things are so miraculous.

Laski: Yes, and yet sometimes people rediscover simplicity through excess. I'm not morally disagreeing with what you are saying but I am wondering whether this—to put forward such a moral point as you do—isn't to impose guilt on most of us who are not so austere. This would be a general charge, not against you only.

Bloom: Guilt is always wrong and guilt is a sickly attitude to life. It's useless. It's destructive and it does away with the very sense that all things are possible, that one can put things right. No, I believe that guilt is wrong but I think that it is a challenge of greater joy. If I say, for instance, I won't do this because I can have the joy of sharing, instead of parasitically, in a predatory way, devouring it for myself, I'm not diminishing my joy and I'm not developing a sense of guilt.

Laski: The only thing I'd say is that if you are wrong—guilty— have done wrong, it's better to bear it yourself than to put it on to other people. It may be necessary to bear your own guilt and work through it.

Bloom: I think it's better to leave the word guilt alone and *do* something. . .

Laski: Certainly, do something, but don't push it on to somebody else.

Bloom: I don't see any advantage in pushing it on somebody else except if somebody is prepared, in terms of affection, friendship, love or whatever you call it, I mean relatedness to you, to share with you your problem, your predicament, not your sense of guilt, not your drowning, but your getting out of it.

Laski: I've been pushing my questions at you and you've been very generous, but have I left out—I'm sure I have—some important area that you would like to put forward? Have I given you insufficient scope to say what's really important to you?

Bloom: No, I think it was very exciting as it was. We never can cover all the ground, anyhow. What I feel, to put it in two very short statements about God and religion, is that to me God is not someone I need to fill gaps. It's someone I have got to accept because from the experience of life I have He does exist; I can't avoid the fact. And the second thing is that all the morals that develop from His existence are part not of a duty to Him or a duty to people—I don't like the word duty—but an act of happiness and gratitude for God and for people, and that links with worship—a worshipful attitude to God, a worshipful attitude to people, a worshipful attitude to life; I think the sense of worship and joy and of a challenge which will make me grow into a full stature is really what matters in practical life.

II

Bloom: What strikes me in the discussion we had before is that we are both on a level of conviction and belief. That is, I said that I had some sort of evidence that God exists. What is your evidence that he does not exist? On what do you base your belief?

Laski: I think I've got to put it in a more negative way. I see no evidence that God exists. No reason to believe that God exists. What you take as evidence seems to me not to count as evidence, not to be sufficient evidence.

Bloom: You call that over-belief—?

Laski: Over-belief? I would say that undoubtedly you and people like you know a feeling that seems as if something that might be called God could exist, but this seems to me to be a feeling that something it might be useful to call God exists, not evidence that God exists. It seems to me more probably to be a feeling of it than true evidence.

Bloom: Where do you draw the line between evidence that is something that does exist and the superstructure which we'll call over-belief? How do you distinguish the one and the other?

Laski: That is a difficult question, but I suppose that evidence would be something that if accepted as valid made a difference to one's entire mental patterning, something that had to be taken into account and which, if not taken into account, falsified every previous picture you'd held of how the world was, how it was constructed. I would rather find, I think, that to believe that God exists in supererogatory. Isn't it William of Occam who said you shouldn't multiply entities unnecessarily? I don't see a need to believe that God exists, or that if I did my picture of the world would be improved. In fact, I think my picture of the world would be falsified in that I would tend to make overtidy patterns about how things are if I believe that God exists, instead of confronting the much greater difficulties that seem to me to be there when I can't accept this.

Bloom: Yes, I see. But is an experience valid when it says to you God does exist? Can you invalidate that kind of statement?

Laski: It doesn't seem to me to be a valid statement at all because there are all kinds of statements I can make from my experience. I can say at a moment of loving infatuation: 'This person is the person I shall be happy with all my life. He is the most beautiful, wonderful creature in the world.' But my eyes are blinded. Or I may have a fever and be hallucinated. Or the sun may shine and I may have an improper optimism about a situation. Or the sun may not shine and I may have an improper pessimism. Surely experience must be tempered by authority, just as authority must be tempered by experience, but on experience alone, I may be mad.

Bloom: That's the kind of thing which the atheists and the believers say about one another quite freely, so we can both accept that kind of qualification. But what is the basic difference between saying 'I know that God exists' and saying 'I know that love exists'?

Laski: I don't think I would say 'I know that love exists' because I wouldn't use abstract words like this. I would say I know several different kinds of feelings that are called love, and it would be better, I think, if we restricted the word a bit more and used it for rather fewer feelings than rather many, but I can certainly say I know various feelings that people call love and I probably don't know all the feelings that people call love. For instance, I don't know your feeling of love of God in any adult sense.

Bloom: What if I simply denied the fact that love does exist, that there is such feeling—whatever the nuance you give it—I suppose you would say there is something lacking in me?

Laski: But haven't you changed the words a bit? I say I know a feeling that it's reasonable to call love, just like I know a feeling of being right and a feeling of being wrong, but I wouldn't myself—I may be only quibbling with words—find it useful to say love exists, right exists, wrong exists. I know what it is to feel loving, let me put it that way, I know what it is when people are feeling loving towards me.

Bloom: Yes I see. But it's an irrational feeling, something which is pure feeling which you accept as an experience without assuming that at the back of it there is such a thing as love, as it were.

Laski: No. You seem to be using irrational there as a rude word.

Bloom: On the contrary.

Laski: But it's a feeling that has all kinds of validations hasn't it? I mean, for instance, you can observe my behaviour when I say I feel loving and say: 'Is my behaviour consonant with what counts as feeling loving?' And if I say I am feeling loving when in fact my eyes are glazed, my hands are cold, I have no energy, you would then be justified in saying: 'Well she may call this love but I think she's mad.' There are references for feeling loving, aren't there?

Bloom: Yes. You moved from some sort of child's belief into unbelief . . . . . or is it too personal a question, how did you make the move into discarding God? Simply by the fact that there was no evidence that satisfied your more adult mind?

Laski: Would you agree that a child's belief in God need have very little to do with an adult's belief in God, except when the adult comes to God he'll make a recognition? This is what was presented to me as God when I was a child and now I can see more clearly. I see that it was right to present this to me. The God I knew and loved as a child was a God presented to me by my parents and He was an imaginary friend, as many children have, and I think I had the same kind of belief in Him that I had, say, in the fairies or that I had, say, in that somewhere there was a country called China. These were all things that came by authority and had to stand the test of time.

Bloom: So it wasn't a God whom you would have said you had met in a sort of intimate relationship. It was a God whom someone else had met and about whom you had been told?

Laski: A little more than that because I think every child's imaginary friend is somebody you meet in a personal relationship and I was certainly very convinced that this God whom I loved was on my side, so to speak. That when my parents said *this* was right and I thought, no, *that* was right, God was with me not with them.

Bloom: You find, say in the Bible, in the Gospels in particular, a sort of poetic evidence but no sort of objective evidence?

Laski: No objective evidence of the existence of God but an objective evidence of the kind of reasons that led people to believe in God and, of course, a great many statements of permanent validity without which I couldn't live nearly so well as I try to.

Bloom: But do you think one can have a convincing poetic

evidence which is founded on nothing but hallucination or nothing but fantasy or wishful thinking?

Laski: Now you are using rude words and unnecessarily because it seems to me that religion would not have existed in every community we know of unless it corresponded to people's deepest needs which couldn't in other ways be satisfied and when you say poetic, we in our post-Renaissance world, take poetry as being something fairly slight compared with religion. But I would have thought that religion was the expression of something we had so far no other means of expressing, something that is to do with our whole best development as human beings, and so when I say I accept this as a poetic myth it's not to denigrate it; in fact it's rather greedily and jealously to say what can I learn from it and in what ways human beings can without the mythical basis of the myth still continue to develop in a life that's a continuance from this and not a break from it.

Bloom: When I think of poetry as far as the human scene is concerned, I always feel that it carries weight, it makes sense because it is an expression in its own terms of something so profoundly real that poetry is the only medium which can be used to transmit the experience or to share it, but what makes it so convincing, so powerful is that there is a reality, human reality, at the root of it.

Laski: But here we agree. I mean I think we were almost reaching the point of difference before, ... if you would say that poetry is an expression of a very deep human reality I am not away from you at all. It's when you suggest, if you are going to suggest, that there is something outside, something other, that we would disagree. It seems to me in fact that the subject of poetry, to take poetry literally now, that the subject that is most often used in poetry is the subject of this very deep emotional pattern-making, in some way closely related to a religious experience, that this is the thing poetry is most about.

Bloom: So that the human experience is genuine and the way it is interpreted you would feel is beyond the evidence as it were, the loss of words, imagination or fantasy.

Laski: Beyond the evidence but not destructively beyond the evidence if one is able to accept it as mythical. We met before on television, I think a year ago, and I remember saying to you I understand you. I still believe that I understand you and I think perhaps this is what I am trying to say, that nothing that you put forward seems to me to be alien or strange but rather to be poetry in its deepest sense.

Bloom: And you would accept, for instance, that passages of the Gospel, to take the Gospel as an example, as being humanly true, without implying that it goes beyond the human truth of it.

Laski: I would not only take them, I would seek them and use them.

Bloom: Because you mentioned the Lord's Prayer, for instance . . . What does the Lord's Prayer mean, apart from the God whom you call 'Our Father' in the beginning, or about Whose kingdom, will and so on you speak? Is it an incantation? You said that you used it.

Laski: Yes, it's hard to say because its meaning changes from one pondering to another. You must find this too. And, except for using it as I think I do in a somewhat incantatory way, it wouldn't be perhaps the words that would most come to my lips, except for this purpose. I mean some of it I would accept, some I would reject. For instance: 'Lead us not into temptation' or, as it says in the New English Bible 'Do not bring us to the test'. This I would reject. This seems to me to be cowardly, but, on the other hand, the pious wish: 'Thy Kingdom Come' this seems an expression of Glory, this is splendid, this is life-giving.

Bloom: My difficulty is not so much such-and-such a sentence but the fact that the Lord's Prayer, for instance, is addressed to someone. If the someone doesn't exist at all, how does it affect you?

Laski: I don't know the answer to that. I mean there is maybe still a childish recourse to a someone. I don't think there often is. Maybe I'm using your image. Could I produce another text, perhaps which I might find easier? One I often think of: 'I Will

Lift up Mine Eyes to the Hills from Whence Cometh My Help'. Now this is more meaningful to me because the help that comes from looking at hills, to those of us who are helped by looking at hills, is a very real thing. We don't know, it may be, as people have said, something to do with the shape of the hills, whatever it may be, but I don't need then to assume a someone, a something that moves on the mountains. I just know, as a human being, that looking at hills is good for many human beings. It helps.

Bloom: I can't see that. My difficulty was that a prayer is addressed to someone or to a void and then I would feel that if there is a void towards which it is addressed then I couldn't use it.

Laski: In moments of deep distress and disaster where it would be natural to pray, in that sense I can't pray and this is one of the things we atheists must do without. I can see that it could be the greatest of strength and comfort to feel you could address a prayer and this perhaps is why I think people address prayers, but we can't do it.

Bloom: My feeling about it is not so much that there is someone to whom you can address a prayer but that the God who I believe exists, makes sense, and is a key of harmony even when the whole piece of music is totally discordant. Where is your key of harmony? Or is the world completely nonsensical?

Laski: Perhaps there isn't a harmony but certainly I think that the attempt to impose a harmony goes far beyond anything we have a right, on what evidence we have, to do. But we can seek for harmony in ourselves, harmony in our surroundings. We can seek the things that give us harmony. This I think is our duty. This is an important thing to do, but to say there is a great ... a universal, an overall harmony, no, I think this is something we impose and God is one of the means by which we impose it.

Bloom: I won't say that there is one, but I would say that we are in a dynamic process of disharmony and tragedy that is aiming at and moving towards a final resolution, a meaning. How can you build meaning on the sort of patchwork which is life day by day?

Laski: First, I wouldn't seek for anything in the nature of a final resolution because that would seem to me to be atrophy and death. The play, as you put it, of a movement towards tragedy and disorder, a movement towards harmony, is the very ebb and flow out of which creativity comes; but meaning, in any large sense, isn't something I would look for, no. I don't understand what this means.

Bloom: What do you feel of life then? You just exist, you act according to—I wouldn't say principles—but to promptings . . .

Laski: Experience and authority—my experience, as purely as I can get it, the best authority I can find to try to be a good animal, a good human being, to the best of my capacity in my society, making as many choices as I feel it's in me to make, reconciling myself where I can't choose.

Bloom: And what about this scale of values? Is there such a thing as a scale of values between things bad and good, better or worse, ugliness and beauty? Is there any sort of base on which one can build a scale of values?

Laski: I've got to be very simple here because what I go by is as easy as comes. What makes me feel better is good. What makes me feel worse is bad. But authority must come in. You see, again, I could be mad. I could be a sadist. If I feel better at beating a child then I must defer to authority. There's something wrong with me, I should go to a doctor. But what makes me feel better, in society, as a social animal, I think, if tested by authority—and part of the authority I could certainly use would be the authority of religion—what tends towards health, the health of me in my society, is good. What tends to unhealth is bad.

Bloom: Yes, but health and unhealth are very relative notions.

Laski: Need they be? Just as you, as a doctor, as you have been, can recognize a state of greater or lesser physical health, surely we are moving towards a point where we are able to recognise a larger kind of health than that, a health. . . a social health for instance as a community, a psychosomatic health of the individual as a whole and one of the things we should be able to do in ourselves, and always with this check of authority, is to know what's good for us and the word good is quite important there, to know what's bad for us.

Bloom: What troubles me is that for instance that in the case where the physical well-being of people has improved they feel happier and yet often I feel so sorry for them because they are missing something more important and I would rather be back to more misery but be alive in the way I was than be more stable, more happy, more satisfied and less dynamically alive.

Laski: I don't think this is wiped out by what I've said. Are you saying better Socrates dissatisfied than the pig satisfied? I think the polarity between unhappiness and happiness, between ill-health and good health, between stagnation and movement, all this is what makes for movement and creativity. And so the last thing I would be saying is that I want to be in a state of perfect endless bliss because this would be similar to your final harmony. You know the atheist poet, William Cory, who said: 'Your chilly heavens I can forego, this warm, kind world is all I know', and the chilly heavens do indeed seem to me to be the area of cold movementlessness like an icy sea.

Bloom: I don't think that harmony is bound to be a stagnation or immobility. When, for instance, you spin a top, there is a moment when the movement is so perfect and intense that it coincides with complete poise.

Laski: But your harmony—I mean if we are talking about music —the harmony of music is made by playing on your nerves, by the exacerbation of discords, by the expectation that isn't fulfilled. There's no peace but the grave.

Bloom: True, there is no peace but in the grave, but I don't see harmony as a grave. What do you think of the people who are sure that there is an otherness which they call God, how do you take into account their experience or what they assert? Do you think that all of them were completely mistaken in their judgment or hallucinated?

Laski: You lead me to the besetting sin of the atheist which is arrogance, so I think I have to say I don't know. I guess there to be a temperamental difference. I guess there to be a difference between people who prefer a minuscule putting together of pieces that may never reach a whole and people like Plato, perhaps, who saw a perfection in ideals. There do seem to me to be people who yearn for an otherness and people who yearn for a here and now, and this is not to make judgment between them but to say that perhaps it's something to do with the way your brain works.

Bloom: Yes, but you spoke of authority as one of the bases for decision and thought. If you take the total authority of mankind in the sense that it occupies a place which seems to be discordant with another line, with the line you have taken, do you feel you need integrate them somehow or would you say, as an atheist once said to me: 'Your belief comes either from hopeless ignorance, *or*, from the fact that you are a crack-pot and as you are not hopelessly ignorant'—or rather he thought I was hopeless but he didn't think I was sufficiently ignorant—'then you must be a hopeless crack-pot.'

Laski: When I said authority I wasn't thinking again of authority for a great big thing, but for little things. 'The hedgehog knows one big thing and the fox knows many things.' I'm a fox. You're a hedgehog. So when I refer to authority, I want to know what authority has said about charity, what authority has said about adultery, what authority has said about lies and anger. But not what it's said about God. It simply seems to me that where these human problems are concerned, what should I do? How should I behave? How can I find consolation? The Fathers of the Church and the Fathers of the Synagogue have been into all this and they've found answers that suit human beings, so there is likely to be an answer that suits me. I don't have to take their source of their answer, but their answer is very likely to suit my condition.

Bloom: I find it surprising because in our time particularly people are so interested in knowing all that exists—travelling and having seen, having read, having heard, being aware of the total reality. My question about this reality is that I feel God is perhaps part of this reality or is not and it's not immaterial to know whether He exists any more than it is immaterial to know whether something else of the material world exists. It's as important in a way, not for a world outlook, but for the sake of my passionate interest in what there is.

Laski: But I have said I don't think God exists. How would my life be changed if I thought otherwise? How would my very imperfect world picture be made more perfect, how would my life be different?

Bloom: What is the difference for your life to have discovered that music exists? In a way, you could very well live without ever having had any experience of music. It may not have made you any better, any worse, but it's an enrichment. It is part of a real and wider experience of life and that's how I would put the problem about God.

Laski: I see this. But surely God doesn't exist for my enrichment. You're suggesting almost that there's another art form I haven't come across. I'm tone deaf to God and I would have a richer life, just as I might if I could understand another art that I don't understand. But God must be something more than this.

Bloom: And yet, as far as my human experience is concerned, when in times past I've said: 'I've no use for music, I am not interested and I dislike it', people have said: 'Oh poor one. You miss so much and you are short of part of life.'

Laski: But at least you knew that music existed. You could watch us listening to it. You could see these people scraping away.

Bloom: With great thought and meditation. . . But what about us scraping away? What about, say, the great people like St Theresa?

Laski: I don't go greatly for St Theresa, because it seems to me that whenever she didn't find people who would agree with her exact interpretation of God, she sought for another adviser, so she is not my favourite saint. But I think she's a good example because she, more than most people, actually believed she perceived God beyond the point which Christianity allows in fact and yet she did not really submit her visions to authority. As I say, she changed her authority whenever it didn't suit her vision.

Bloom: Yet here is a woman and here are many people who possess something they say is real. And you would go a long way to discover a new writer, a new artist, in terms of painting or sculpture, a new world of discovery and yet you would say this is not worth investigating and discovering. That's what puzzles me.

Laski: I don't think I'm saying that. I would certainly probably not have investigated it so far as you would think proper. It's certain that I don't see any substitute for this world of yours because since the Renaissance for instance, it's been all too sadly apparent that in all the arts there has been no inspiration comparable with the inspiration that religion gave. There have been no words for secular music that compare with the music of a Mass. I certainly think that belief in God and the religions that arose from belief in God did give a shaping and a pattern to life for which I can see no conceivable substitute and to that extent I would certainly grant to you that my life is poorer than that of a believer. My justification for it, and I say it as humbly as I can, is that it's founded on the truth as I see it and the truth has to make me free of perfection. I'm not entitled to it.

Bloom: I feel terribly happy about what you said because I think what really matters first of all is integrity and truth and I'm certain that if God exists, which I believe He does, He's happier about truth of unbelief than falsified belief. Now I think I must give you the chance you gave me to say what you would like to say in addition to our discussion.

Laski: I probably haven't made atheism seem at all rich and I don't think it is. I think it's a very Protestant, a very puritanical faith that, as I say, does tend towards arrogance because we lack authority. But there is one thing I would say for atheism, as against religion, and that is this: if you try to practice it, it trains you in a virtue that I value highly which is endurance without whimpering and without seeking help you can't properly expect to have. But we must—I say 'we', I don't know who 'we' are, I don't know who atheists are and this is, again, where arrogance comes in—but we must depend very deeply on religions which have a great many things that we can't have—rite, ritual, festival, words beyond any words we've managed to maintain. I think sometimes that we could have more help.

CHAPTER TWO

DOUBT AND THE CHRISTIAN LIFE[1]

I DO NOT mean to give a complete exposition of Christianity. I want to take a certain number of points which I think are relevant for the Christian and which are relevant for anyone who wishes to understand himself and the situation in which we as Christians find ourselves. Perhaps when I say 'we Christians' I go beyond the limits of what I should say; perhaps I should say 'the way in which one Christian who belongs to the Russian Church understands it', because it will be a personal contribution. It is offered not as a teaching but to stimulate thought.

Periodically there are words that emerge that characterise a situation. When one uses the words 'problem' and 'problematic', one means things that had seemed to be absolutely clear to the generation before but which now have unfolded themselves in a new way and have acquired a depth of vision which requires new thinking. We are no longer content with a simple repetition of views which belonged to a previous generation. I am talking about such things as the historical meaning of tragic events like the Russian Revolution, suffering—communal or family—and national tragedies.

Nowadays it seems that the words which come easily to mind are *bewilderment, perplexity,* and they result in an attitude of mind because the trouble with words is that they begin by defining a situation that exists and then they try to crystallise the

---

[1] Chapters two, three, and five are edited versions of talks given at Birmingham University in 1970.

situation, making out of it a sort of world outlook. People confronted with a problem are perplexed; they say so, and that is right. Later, however, people have come to the perplexity before the problem and think that they are up to date if they are perplexed, but that doesn't always lead to a solution.

Therefore, before we start to consider anything more concrete in our faith or world outlook, I would like to focus attention on perplexity and on doubt, in an attempt to provoke thought about a few words like faith, doubt, reality and truth. I am not a theologian; I am a scientist by training and a physician, so you will not find in my words any depth of philosophical probing into things. I am writing as an ordinary human being who is confronted with life and its problems.

First of all, concerning faith, one preliminary remark. Faith is very often understood by people as a defeat of intelligence. In other words, faith begins when I can no longer think creatively, when I let go of any attempt at rational understanding, and when I say 'I believe' because it is so absurd that it is the only way of facing the problem. This may be an act of credulity, it may be an act of cowardice, it may be a preliminary act, full of wisdom and intelligence, that teaches us not to draw conclusions or to come to conclusions before we have understood. But this is not faith as understood by the great men of all religions, and particularly the Christian faith. In the Epistle to the Hebrews in the eleventh chapter, faith is defined as 'certainty of things unseen'. We usually lay the stress on 'things unseen' and forget the 'certainty' about them. So when we think of faith we usually think of the invisible and instead of certainty put against it an interrogation mark. Then to solve the problem, we accept in a childish way, in an unintelligent way very often, what we are told by others—usually our grandparents of three generations back, or whoever else we choose to believe for reasons that are not always reasonable. But if you try to see the way in which faith originates in those people who were the great men of faith, the heroes of faith, you can see that it always originates in an experience that makes the invisible certain, and which allows them, having discovered that the invisible is as real as the visible, to go further in searching the invisible by methods of their own.

There is a passage for instance, in the works of Macarius of Egypt, a man who lived in the fourth century. He says 'The experience of God, the vision of the world in God, is something which can happen only at a moment when all our thoughts, all emotions, are arrested to such a degree that we can no longer both be within the experience, perceive the things, and step out of the experience, watch ourselves and analyse what is going on. The moment when an experience is "lived" is a moment when we cannot observe it.' And he says that this would be quite sufficient for someone who has had an experience of God. He would not wish to go back to another stage. But he also says, 'God has concern, not only for those who have this experience, but also for the people who haven't got it; that someone should come to them as a witness of things unseen, and yet experienced, real, and he steps back away from them.' At that moment begins, as he says, the realm of faith. The certitude remains even though the experience is already of the past; the certainty is there because what has happened to him is as certain as anything around him, is tangible, visible, perceived by the senses, so that the moment of faith begins as a result of a first contact with the invisible, discovered, disclosed somehow.

That means that we must be very severe and sober when we speak of our faith, for we often say 'I believe this and that' when we have taken it from someone else that it is true—we don't care to investigate it in depth, and as long as this truth or illusory truth is not destroyed or broken down, then we take it for granted. This is a bad faith; this is what one of our Russian theologians called 'the aged sacrament of the faith that does not think'.

What we *should* do whenever we are faced with that kind of faith is to confront it with experience. We ask ourselves whether we have any experience of it. If we haven't, it must remain a field to be investigated. It remains a field that was conveyed to us by someone who knows, but which is not known to us. It is promising, but it must hold its promise in the future. We cannot yet say 'I know, I am certain, I understand with experience.'

This kind of faith—the faith of one who simply takes things on trust—sooner or later will be badly battered by life and by problems, by doubt in fact, or if you prefer, by perplexity. What happens so often with people is that when they are young, they are given a number of certainties which they accept on trust from their parents, their teachers, their surrounding, the milieu in which they live. After that, this minimum of faith is kept as a sort of treasure. We develop in all sorts of ways, but our awareness of the world invisible and of the certainties it entails does not grow with it. A moment comes round the age of 18, perhaps earlier or later, when a child in us, the little child of 8 who has collected all the faith he was capable of and formed a world outlook which is childish, is confronted with an opponent, an adversary within himself. A girl, a young man, of 18, 20 or 25, says 'Nonsense, you can't believe that', and then an argument starts which is doomed to lead to the defeat of faith simply because it is the argument between a little child with a pure heart and uninvolved thinking, against someone who poses to the childish nature the problems of another age, another level of understanding, another level of perception of the world.

At 8 the world can be taken on trust; at 18, at 25, it cannot; and in certain circumstances, there are things that can never be taken on trust. I will give you an example. The Eucharist, the central event of Christian worship, is centred on an act of thanksgiving in which we say to God 'Thank you for all things'. Now, can we honestly say, 'thank you for all things' in the face of the tragedies of the world unless we have a reason to see beyond the tragedy to their solution and a meaning within them?

Doubt is not simply contradiction. Doubt is a moment of dividedness, a dichotomy in our minds; a moment when, having followed a very simple straight road, we come to a fork, and we ask ourselves 'Do I go this way or that way?' The one may be more convincing, the other may be more alluring. Which one are we going to choose? It is the situation of someone who has been weighing up the problems of life in a very simple way and suddenly discovers there is a much more subtle balance between things and that a simple solution is no solution at all. What are we going to do at that moment?

There are two absolutely different attitudes to doubt in the mind—there is that of the scientist and that of the believer. For the scientist, doubt is a systematic weapon; it is a joy. For the believer when he takes the wrong attitude to doubt and to the problems he is facing, it is a moment of anguish. What happens usually to the believer is that having believed in all simplicity that everything is clear, simple, straightforward, he suddenly discovers that life gives the lie to what he thought to be true. Then his answer is 'I am disloyal to what I thought, I am disloyal to my faith, to my Church, to my God'. The problem is not only about subtleties but about basic things, about God Himself, about the Church, about what is at the core of the believer's life. Then he feels that what is at stake is the breaking down, the destruction, the disappearance of the object of faith, and God's existence is now questionable. The values which were essential, which were existential values for him, are questionable, and therefore his very existence becomes a problem and seems to be insuperably problematic.

But when a scientist engages in research, he gathers together all the facts he is capable of collecting. Once he has gathered his facts, he must hold them together in a way that makes it possible for him to handle the totality of the facts, and he builds a hypothesis, a theory, a model, a construction, an architectural building, that is capable of holding everything together. If the whole object of research for the scientist was to make himself a name, he will try to protect his model against any criticism, against any doubt and against any questioning, with greater or lesser honesty. But if as a scientist he is a man who is out to discover what things are in reality, his first action will be to go round and round his model in all directions, examining and trying to find where the flaw is, what the problems are which are generated by the model he has built, by the theory he has proposed, by the hypothesis he has now offered for the consideration of others. If he cannot find a flaw, then he will try through research to go farther in the field and discover such facts that do not fit with his theory or his model, because when he will find a fact that will explode his model, make his theory questionable, he will have opened up a new window on reality. So the aim of the good research scientist is to create models of theories or hypotheses as a preliminary exercise to questioning and to discovering something which will make him break them down in order to create another model which is as doubtful as the preceding one, but which allows him to keep the new facts together in a manageable way.

At the root of the scientist's activity there is the certainty that what he is doubting is the model he has invented—that is, the way in which he has projected his intellectual structures on the world around him and on the facts; the way in which his intelligence has grouped things. But what he is also absolutely certain of is that the reality which is beyond his model is in no danger if his model collapses. The reality is stable, it is there; the model is an inadequate expression of it, but the reality doesn't alter because the model shakes.

'Model' can be replaced by another word when it is not used in a scientific way—it can be replaced by the word 'truth'. Truth is something which is an expression of reality, and an expression means two things: first, that the reality which surrounds us is perceived (obviously incompletely); secondly, that it is expressed (also incompletely, because of our inability to express identically in words and in expressions). Only one occasion in human history sees the moment when truth and reality coincide. That moment is in the incarnation Christ, because he is God, the plenitude, the fullness of creation, and at the same time the perfect expression of it. Then truth no longer answers the question 'What?', it answers the question 'Who?', and when Pilate said 'What is truth?' Christ gave him no answer for the simple reason that if he had said to him what he had said to the disciples, 'I am the Truth' Pilate would have understood even less than the disciples, and the disciples understood nothing at that particular moment.

Truth and the expression of it is bound to be formulated in human terms, in the language of a given tribe, a nation, an epoch and so forth. Obviously it is limited, but it has also another quality: truth can be either static or dynamic. You can express the truth in two ways. A snapshot is true and yet it is perfectly untrue. Everyone must have seen snapshots of preachers, lecturers or politicians delivering a speech. They are usually taken at a moment when the subjects stand with their mouths open like a hippopotamus. Well, the snapshot is perfectly true, but it expresses only a split second and gives you a ridiculous image of something that perhaps at that moment was profoundly moving for the people. It is a petrification, a sort of fossil of something which is dynamic; it is true, and yet it does not express the truth because the truth at that moment was emotion. When you want to express the truth—that is, reality—dynamically, you discover that the truth becomes a problem of a quite different sort. Perhaps an example or two will explain what I mean.

There is a painting by the French painter Géricault called *The Derby at Epsom*. If you look at the painting, you will see that the horses are galloping, but if you are interested in zoology or in the mechanics of movement and examine the horses, you will discover that no horse gallops that way. Some are spread out in such a way that if they went on they would fall flat on their bellies; others stand with their four feet gathered together and couldn't even jump from the position in which they are painted. But what was Géricault aiming at? He aimed at showing the gallop and not the horses. The problem was to express the movement and not the anatomy, the physiology. And he chose deliberately (because he knew perfectly well how to draw a horse) to falsify things as the only way of convincing the viewer that the horses were moving.

This is what we are always doing in theology or philosophy: we falsify things when we want to convey a dynamic moment, but often the reader takes them to be an adequate and immobile picture of what reality it. This is true, for instance, of the Trinity.

There is another example which I should like to give about reality. It is that of false teeeth. When we say these are false teeth, we are making a judgement of value but not of reality. We start with the common assumption that real teeth grow spontaneously in peoples' mouths. This is true; from this point of view those teeth which you can remove in the evening, wash under the tap and keep in a glass are evidently false. But from the point of view of the dentist, they are perfectly real (false) teeth. It sounds like a joke, but that is the kind of mistake which we make continually. We don't notice it, but we start to speak of something from an angle, move to another and we discover that the two don't work together.

No, reality is something within us which is the total thing

which includes God and all things visible and invisible. This is what we aim at expressing in glimpses when we speak in terms of truth. These terms of truth may be adequate, they are never identical with their object. In the field of art something very interesting may be discovered in the works of primitive painters particularly of one Russian painter called Rublev who lived 600 years ago. He was trained by a man who had mastery of three-dimensional painting, and strangely enough, for most of his painting he reverted to two-dimensional. A Soviet historian of art made a study of the problem, and he showed that Rublev expresses all historical events in three-dimensional, because particularly in time and in space they have thickness. But things which belong to the eternal, he expresses only in two dimensions because they have no thickness—they are not within time and within space. When you look out of the window during the night in a thunderstorm, you may see the scenery in a flash—but it goes so quickly that you can't see whether one tree is farther or nearer than another, or any so precise detail. This is the way that truth is both adequate and inadequate. When we say that the truth is inadequate, that our intellectual, philosophical, theological, scientific model is inadequate in comparison with reality, it simply means that we are saying 'How marvellous, I have come to a point when I can outgrow the limitations in which I have lived and I can move into a greater, deeper, more enthralling vision of things as they are.'

If we think of a scientist and a believer, then we will see that the scientist's doubt is systematic, it is surging, it is hopeful, it is joyful, it is destructive of what he has done himself because he believes in the reality that is beyond and not in the model he has constructed. This we must learn as believers for our spiritual life both in the highest forms of theology and in the small simple concrete experience of being a Christian. Whenever we are confronted with a crossroads, whenever we are in doubt, whenever our mind sees two alternatives, instead of saying 'Oh God, make me blind, Oh God help me not to see, Oh God give me loyalty to what I know now to be untrue', we should say 'God is casting a ray of light which is a ray of reality on something I have outgrown—the smallness of my original vision. I have come to a point when I can see more and deeper, thanks be to God.' That is not perplexity, it is not bewilderment, it is not the anguished doubt of the believer who hides his head and hopes that he will be able to revert to the age of 8.

This is very important because unless you are prepared to see reality and your own thoughts and the thoughts of others with keen interest, with courage, but with the certainty that the last word is not doubt, not perplexity and not bewilderment, but that it is discovery, then you are wasting your time. You will die in the way in which in ancient mythology we are told: an ass that stood between a bucket of water and some straw and could never decide whether he was more hungry than thirsty or more thirsty than hungry.

I should like to talk now of the situation of being a Christian in the world; and I should like to preface my remarks by saying that we have a tendency to exaggerate the meaning which we attach to the expression 'the contemporary world'. The world is always contemporary to someone: at every moment it will be contemporary to a generation of people, and there are general rules that are human and historical which I believe can serve as a basis for our judgement and action. Another thing which I should like to underline is the fact that God is always contemporary. This we very often forget, trying by all sorts of theological efforts to make Him contemporary with us, when He is perfectly contemporary, needs no change to be Himself and to be up to date.

This being said, I take as a first starting point two stories of the Gospel which are too well known for me to describe them in detail—the stories of two storms on the Lake of Galilee. The scheme of these two stories is practically identical. The disciples leave the shore, they are caught up in a storm and they are confronted with the unexpected in the person of their Lord and of their God, Jesus Christ. In the first story the disciples left the shore, then they were caught up in the storm alone in their boat. Christ had remained behind, dismissing the crowds after the miracle of the multiplication of the bread and fish. Their only protection against the storm was the frail shell of their boat. They

fought with all their energy, with all their skill, with all their
courage, yet death was enveloping them on every side, pressing
hard, trying to break through their precarious security. At a
certain moment they saw, right in the middle of the storm,
walking on the seas, blown around by the wind, Christ himself.
They looked and saw and they cried out in fear because they
knew it could not be Christ, they knew it was a ghost. Why?
Because they knew that God, their God, their Master, their
Teacher, stood for harmony, for peace, for salvation, for life,
and there he was right in the middle of the storm which spelt
death, disharmony and horror; it could not be God, because
God's presence could not be in harmony with what was going on.

This is the reaction we have so often, and we react as wrongly
as the disciples when dramatic events occur in our lives. Whether
it is history at large—wars and earthquakes—whether it is the
small history in which we are involved—our own lives, our
own families, our own religion, colour, group—if the presence
of God is felt and is not accompanied by immediate harmony,
by the coming of peace, by salvation, by the relief of pain and
by the relief of anguish, we shout out that it is a ghost. He cannot
be there. We forget that God is the Lord of the storm just as he
is the Lord of the stillness, the serenity and the harmony of
things.

I will leave this story at this point and take the next one, and
come back to both. In this one we read that Christ has left the
shore with his disciples. He is asleep in the prow of the boat; he
is asleep comfortably, resting his head on a cushion. A storm
springs up, death is abroad, fear enters and conquers the hearts
of the disciples. They fight again within the precarious protection
of the shell of the boat, and they feel that they are being defeated.
Then they turn towards Him who is their salvation, or should be;
and they see Him who should be their salvation completely
indifferent, asleep, at rest, and—to add insult to injury—he is not
only asleep but he has made himself comfortable with his head
on a cushion.

This is what we accuse God of continuously. We never stop
accusing him of that. We are fighting against death; anguish
disrupts our lives; fear makes them unbearable; death is abroad,

suffering is killing us, and God is not only there, indifferent, but in perfect comfort because he is beyond reach of these things. Are we fair and are we right? I will try to answer this question a little later. Let us go back to more features of the story.

In the first story, having cried out their fear, the disciples hear the Lord say 'Fear not, it is I'. They hear a voice which is strangely like the familiar and loved voice of their master. And Peter acting once more quickly than he thinks, says, 'If it is you, tell me to walk on the seas and join you'. And then, because Christ says 'Yes, it is I, come', Peter of a sudden—because he has recognised Him who is life, who is meaning, who is harmony, in himself—of a sudden abandons the frail protection of their boat, and begins to walk and indeed he walks, and as long as he looks at Christ, and as long as his only desire is to be with Him, to be at that point where God stands in the storm, he can walk. But suddenly he remembers himself. He remembers that he is a man of flesh and blood, that he has gravity, that he has never walked on the sea, never withstood the raging waves, that he will drown; and the moment he turns his gaze, his interest, his concern on himself, he indeed begins to drown because he is still in that part of the storm where death is abroad.

In the case of the second story, the disciples feel defeated—death is there, they have no strength left, no hope, no peace left. Turmoil has overcome them completely; they turn to him, they awake him, perhaps even brutally, for their words are brutal. 'For all you care, we are dead'. This is the translation which Moffatt gives of that passage. 'For all you care, we are dead'. They don't turn to him saying, 'You are the Lord, a word of yours will be sufficient for us to be saved'. No, they recognise defeat, they accept the ruthlessness and indifference of God, they have no word for Him. What they want of this God become man who proves incapable of being a help and their salvation, if he can do nothing better, is to be in anguish, in despair, together with them and to die with them—not be drowned unconsciously, all unwitting of the oncoming defeat of life by death. And Christ turns away from them, brushes them away saying 'How long shall I be with you, men of little faith?' Then, turning to the storm, he commands the seas to be still and the wind to cease, projecting as it were, his own serenity, his own peace, his own stillness, his own harmony, on all things around Him. In the case of Peter as well as in the case of the other apostles, they had allowed the storm not only to rage around them, but to enter into them; the storm had become an internal experience; it had conquered. In Christ it remains outside himself; it is conquered. In a passage of St John's Gospel, the Lord says 'the Prince of the world has nothing in him which he can use to kill'. They are not His words but the implication is that He is free, He has overcome the world; he can project on it the measurement, the categories of eternity, stability, serenity, salvation, security, not the precarious and frail security of the little boat, but another security; not the peace, the naive peace of those who say 'That will never happen to me', or console others by saying 'Don't worry it won't happen to you', but the peace of one who has said 'It may happen, it will happen, it has happened, and yet because I have lost all human hope, I stand firm and unshaken on divine hope.'

I have said that Christ was at the point of a storm, at a certain point of the storm which we should reach in order to be with God in the storm; that Peter nearly drowned because he did not reach it. Where is this point? This point of the storm is not a point where there is no storm, it is what one calls the eye of the hurricane, it is the point where all conflicting forces meet and where an equipoise is reached because there is no violence—not because there is no tension, not because there is no tragedy, but because the tragedy and the tension have come to such a pitch that they meet so violently as to balance each other; they are at the point of breaking. This is the point where God stands, and when we think of God, the God of history, the God of human life, the God whom we accuse all the time, to whom we give from time to time a chance by saying 'He must be right because he is God'—this is the God who has chosen to stand at the breaking point of things, and this is why He can be respected, why we can treat Him with consideration, why we can believe in Him and not despise Him.

Now, where is this point? Long ago a man once stood in anguish, in despair, before the face of God and before the judgement of his friends. This man was called Job. He was afflicted with all that can afflict a man—bereavement, loss of all he possessed, loss of all that was dear, but more than this, more tragically than this, with the loss of understanding. He no longer could understand his God. Meaning had gone out of his life, and in his argument with God and in his argument with his friends, he stood for meaning and refused consolation; he refused to be consoled and got out of tragedy and anguish by a consoling, appeasing and false image of God and of his ways. He believed, indeed he knew a living God, and that one he could no longer understand. And at a certain moment, he says, 'Where is the man that will stand between me and my judge, who will put his hand on my shoulder and on my judge's shoulder; where is he that will step into the situation, take a place at the heart of the conflict, at the breaking point of the tension, stand between the two in order to re-unite them, and to make them one?' He had a sense that only that could be the solution of his problem. Indeed of the problem of the meaning of tragedy, ultimately of the meaning of history. He had a foreboding that only that could be true, and that indeed happened. It happened when the Son of God became the Son of Man, when the Word of God became flesh, when Jesus came into the world, who being truly man, could put his hand on the man's shoulders without destroying the man by the fire of divine touch, and who could without blasphemy and sacrilege, put his hand on the shoulder of God without being destroyed.

This is what we truly mean by Intercession. Christians spend their time interceding, and at times I listen to these intercessions with fear because to me intercession means an involvement that may spell death; and I am frightened when I hear a congregation of people intercede for one need after the other, piling up on their shoulders all the needs of the world just for the time Evensong lasts. After that they put it down on God's shoulders, and they go out elevated with a new emotion.

About ten years ago I came back from India. I was asked in London to speak at a rather big meeting about hunger. I spoke about what I had seen and what had wounded me very deeply with all the passion and violence I am capable of. For a while

the people sat and listened, then when we came out I stood at
the west door shaking hands, and a lady came up to me and
said 'Thank you for the entertaining evening.' That is intercession very often with us. We have spied a need, we have become
aware of a tragedy, and then from the security of our living, we
turn to God, and say 'O Lord, haven't you noticed that? What
are you doing about it? And this? And that? Aren't you forgetful
of your duties to mankind? This is not intercession. Intercession
is a Latin word which means to take a step that brings you to the
centre of the conflict, and in the image of Christ, in the person of
Christ, we see that intercession means taking a step which is
definitive—once and for all he becomes man, not for a while.
And he doesn't become a pleading advocate or a go-between
equally different to the one on either side, who will go and find
terms of agreement between the one and the other. He takes his
stand in total, final solidarity between Man and God; turning
to God, he is man and stands condemned; turning to men he is
God and stands rejected. He must die. And his solidarity doesn't
go simply to the sweet selected few who will recognise him or
believe in him. No, his solidarity goes to everyone. He is not God
for the good versus the bad, the believers versus the unbelievers,
or the creed or the colour of a nation, or of a social group. He
has made himself solid with everyone. We discovered as exiled
Russians in the early days of emigration when we had lost
everything, when there was nothing left standing for us, when we
were unwanted, rejected, despised, helpless, vulnerable to the
utmost, we discovered we had also lost the God of the great
cathedrals, the God of the beautifully engineered ceremonials.
Where did we stand? When we looked at ourselves, we discovered
that we had lost faith in ourselves, and very often self-respect.
And then we discovered our God in a new way. We discovered
that in Christ God has revealed himself as vulnerable, as helpless,
as contemptible, as overcome and vanquished, as trodden under
foot, as rejected, and we discovered that we had a God who was
not ashamed of us, because he had made Himself solid with what
we were, in our misery, in our deprivation, in our rejection, and
also that we had no reason to be ashamed of a God who knew
how to love to the extent that he was prepared to become one of

us, and to show by doing this that his faith in us was unshaken and that his respect of human dignity was whole and untouched.

This God is the one who stands at the middle of history. He is the one who stands at the breaking point of the storm, and he calls us to stand where He stands, to be involved, to be committed, to be committed to life and death within the storm, and yet neither to accept this fallacy of a ghost in the storm instead of God, or to turn to God and say 'If you can do nothing more, at least be together with us, in anguish and in despair'. He wants us to take a step, to be in the world at the point which I called 'the eye of the hurricane', but not *of* the world, because we are free from the uncertainty, from the fear, from the self-centredness of Peter, remembering himself at a moment when the whole sea was death and danger for the other disciples, for all the other boats around, and when God stood there as the key of harmony, but it was not the harmony that he expected.

I should like to give you one example of what it means both to make an act of intercession and to stand where our place is. It is the story of a woman of whom we know nothing except the name. She was called Natalie. The story was told me by the other people involved in it. In 1919 at a moment when the Civil War was raging like a storm over Russia, when our cities were falling prey to one army after the other, a woman with two young children was trapped in a city which had fallen into the hands of the Red Army, while her husband was an officer of the White Army. To save her life and theirs, she hid in a small cabin at the outskirts of the city. She wanted to wait until the first surges were over and try to escape afterwards. On the second day someone knocked at her door towards the evening. She opened it in fear and she was confronted with a young woman of her age. The woman said 'You must flee at once because you have been discovered and betrayed; you will be shot tonight'. The other woman, showing her children that stood there, said, 'How could we do that? We would be recognised at once, and they can't walk far.' The young woman who so far had been nothing but a neighbour, someone living next door, became that great thing which one calls a neighbour in the Gospel. She grew to the full stature of the Gospel of God, of the good news of the dignity and graciousness of man, and she said 'They won't look for you, I shall stay behind.' And the mother said 'But they will kill you.' 'Yes', said the woman, 'but I have no children, you must go.' And the mother went.

It is not easy, I would say it is almost sacrilegious, to try to imagine what happened in the heart and mind of this woman in the course of the hours that preceded her death. But we can look back to the Gospel and see what happened in the Gospel to those who were the prototype, the archetype of this great and holy woman.

Almost two thousand years before, a young man of her age was waiting for his death. His name was Jesus. He was in a garden wrapped in the darkness of the coming night. There was no reason within him why he should die. He was young, healthy; he had done nothing wrong. He was waiting to die in a vicarious way other peoples' death. He was waiting in the darkness of the night, and death was coming to kill life eternal itself. Three times he went towards his disciples, hoping for a word that would strengthen his heart, for companionship: not to be released, not to be saved from the oncoming death, but to feel that there was a human presence, compassion, love and awe. The disciples were asleep. He got no help.

Natalie in the coming night, in the gathering darkness, in the cold that was falling from the walls and the roof, had nowhere to turn; there was no-one to whom she could turn. She was alone, facing the coming of another woman's death that would be enacted in her body, in her destiny. She could have walked out. The moment she had passed the threshold, she was again Natalie, not the mother. Two thousand years before on that same cold night when Christ was betrayed into the hands of his murderers, the strongest, the most daring of his disciples was challenged three times, twice by a little maid in the courtyard, once by a group of standers-by; he was not asked 'Are you Jesus?' he was told 'You were with him!' and three times he said 'No', and walked out of the courtyard. Into what? Into security. He turned round and the eyes of Christ met his eyes, and he remembered and he wept. But he walked out. Natalie did not walk out, she stayed inside.

How often must she have thought 'Is there any hope that at least my sacrifice will be useful?' Again, two thousand years ago a man was waiting for death, John the Baptist, and before he died, when he knew that death was inevitable, he sent two of his disciples to Christ to ask Him 'Are you He for whom we waited, or shall we expect another one?' That means 'If you are Him, then my life of asceticism, my aloneness, my preaching, my imprisonment and death, all the tragedy and hardship of my life, make sense. But if you are not, then I have been betrayed by God and by man, by my own inspiration and by the weakness of the living God. Are you He?' Christ did not give him a direct answer. He gave him the answer of the prophet 'Go and tell him what you see—the blind see, the lame walk and the poor proclaim the good news—news about God—news about man.' The humility of the one and the greatness of the other.

Natalie probably asked herself the same question—was it in vain that she was dying? There was no answer, only the hours passed, the cold of the early morning came and with it, death. The door was brutally opened and they did not even take the trouble of dragging her out. She was shot where she was.

This is the answer which the Christian can give to the tragedy of history. The place where we must stand. Natalie stood where Christ had stood, and where indeed Christ stands now, risen in Heaven with his hands and sides seared with nails and the spear. He stands at the very heart of human history, human suffering, human death, human anguish and tragedy. But He stands there like a rock. He stands there firm, having endured everything, every human suffering in thought and body, and he says to us Christians, 'That is where you must stand, not in the dreamland of a faith that gives you the illusion that you are already in heaven while you have never been on earth. No, at the heart of human suffering and tragedy but with a faith unshaken, with the certainty that He who was expected by Job, has come'. And if we stand there, we may undergo all that was promised by him. You remember the passage: 'Are you prepared and capable of drinking of the cup which I shall drink, of undergoing what I shall go?' 'Yes', said his two disciples. This must be our answer, and when tragedy comes, we must answer again as Isaiah spoke: ' "Whom shall I send?" said the Lord. "Here I am, send me." ' Like a sheep among the wolves; like the Son of God among men.

CHAPTER THREE

MAN AND GOD

IN THE 18th and 19th centuries, the centre of interest was mainly ideas and ideals, and man was the material support of these ideals or this concept. He was subservient to them, he was supposed to serve them, to live for them and eventually to die for them. There was greatness in this approach and if we forget its significance, we would certainly lose a very important dimension of humanity. Man's greatness is I believe, to be measured, not only by his potentialities but also by his ability to live for and to die for things which in his view are greater than him. But we know also that when ideals and ideas acquire such independence as to become overlords of the minds and lives of people, when men are no longer free to approach them critically, but are forced into one-sidedness that involves them in life and death without any choice of their own, then something has gone wrong. And it is not surprising that nowadays, as a revulsion against what has been happening since the beginning of the First World War, we have a sense of the value and the significance of man in his frailty, in his becoming, in his search, as well as in his achievements and in the service he can render to things great.

Nowadays man is a meeting point of all those who are in search of things true and things right. If St Paul came back into our world and was faced with an altar dedicated to the Unknown God, he might very well say 'I know his name, his name is Man', and at that point he would probably meet not only those who believe but also those whom we call unbelievers. I would like to build part of this chapter on two quotations: the one belongs to Karl Marx and the other one to St John Chrysostom. These are two poles.

Karl Marx says approximately that the society of the worker is in no need of a God because Man has become its God, and St John Chrysostom in one of his innumerable sermons says that if you wish to know how great man is, don't turn your eyes towards the thrones of the kings or the palaces of the great men, look up towards the throne of God and you will see the Son of Man seated at the right hand of Glory. In both cases it is man who is the final, the greatest vision, and greatest value.

I would like now to take up not these two quotations, but the vision of man which they imply and see whether the unbeliever, the humanist, the atheist and the Christian have got anything to say to one another about it. If you think of man conceived in atheistic terms—I am not now using the word 'atheistic' to refer to aggression against God, but to an attitude of mind and outlook in which God has no place, in which he doesn't exist—you will see that man appears in various ways. The empirical and concrete man is not the object of the exercise. The concrete man is raw material; this raw material is in the process of *becoming;* from the point of view of natural science it would be called evolution, from the point of view of social science one would speak of an evolving society, but the empirical man is not *the* reality which concerns the atheist uniquely. As raw material he exists, but he is to be set up against a certain number of visions, the first of all of which may be of the man of the future—man as he should become when he will have become what he should be. I remember a discussion I had on a plane between Moscow and the south of Russia with an atheist who said to me that we should not judge the success or failure of the Russian Revolution by what was actually achieved or not achieved as yet, because the result of the revolution will be shown when men will have been transformed in such a way that they become real men. In other words, man is always viewed as something ahead of us, something in the future towards which we move; and the empirical raw material which we all are is to be worked upon, transformed, changed and moulded, and in this recasting, as experience shows through the centuries, many bones crack and many things have to be changed with force and sometimes with violence.

The second aspect of man is society, the present-day society representing a collective vision of man and the empirical man being forced into, led into, or convinced into becoming an integral and harmonious part of the society. The level of the change may of course be valued in different ways. We may think that the society to which this man belongs is far below the mark, and at times, often perhaps, far below the mark of its individual members; but it is society which is the collective man, and the individual man must be fitted in like a little stone in a vast and complex mosaic. In that case also man has to be re-adjusted, re-formed.

Another aspect of the attitude of the unbeliever to man is that the empirical man has a right to be what he is and to become whatever he will become. That, when you think of it in an absolute sense, leads to a vision which is near the vision of the anarchist—everyone has a right to be himself whatever he is—and to the sort of idealistic idea that if everyone was allowed to be nothing but himself, unhampered, the final result would be perfect harmony.

It may also lead in the process to accepting man as he is, not only with his frailty and his becoming, but also with his right to be a problem to his neighbour, to be subservient to his passions, to his weaknesses, to refuse any idealism, any desire for change, and be content with being what he is, however low this level of being may be. I am not speaking of course of a high or low level of living which is not what the empirical man seeks, but the acceptance of himself in his laziness, in his lack of ideals, in his refusal to be part of a whole which is greater than him, and so on.

In the case of society defining man or in the case of an ideal abstract man being set up as the pattern for the future becoming, we always meet—whatever the case, whatever the kind of dictatorship or pressure group—with something which a Russian writer, Solzhenitsyn, in his book *Cancer Ward*, defined in the following way. One of the central characters has this said about him, 'He had the greatest possible love and consideration for mankind, and this is why he hated so fiercely every human being that disfigured this ideal so horribly'. This is exactly what happens when we have no other standard and no other point of reference than either an ideal which we build out of our imagination according to what we desire, or else when it is society, the concrete pack which is around us, which defines what each of the howling wolves should be. Man confronted with an abstract ideal of man or with a concrete, real society which clings to totalitarian rights, must be remoulded, must be broken, must be changed and must be brought—a blood offering very often— to this abstract ideal or perish, confronted with his inability to fit with the pack, the concrete society, the jungle in which he lives.

Christianity also sets men as the final value, but not idealistically or abstractly. We have put on the altar a concrete real man —Jesus of Nazareth—and we must have a look at what is implied. We see in the Creed that Christ was true man and true God. When we say that he was true man we imply two things: the fact that he was God has not made him into a man alien to us, a man so different from us that he has only the same shape and the same name while in reality he has nothing in common with us; on the other hand, we proclaim that being the true man means to be a revelation of man in his fulfilment, man as he is called to be, and that in Christ we have a vision—concrete, real, historical—of what we are called to become in our reality, in our historicity and in our becoming. So when we say that Christ is true man, we affirm that to be united with the Godhead does not annihilate or change the nature of mankind, and it is only in Him because man is united in Him with the Godhead; that man is revealed in his full possibility because man as a specimen of natural history is not man in the sense in which we believe man is truly human. Man becomes truly human only when he is united with God infinitely, deeply, inseparably, so that the fullness of Godhead abides in the flesh. I am using terms which are applied to Christ in the Scriptures, but which I believe are applicable to man if we take, for instance, the words of St Peter in his Epistle that our vocation is to become partakers of the divine nature—God's participation and not just human beings related to a God who remains an outsider to us.

But that implies a quite different vision of man, and it also implies something which I believe to be important, a quite different vision of the Church.

Very often we think of the Church in sociological terms; it is a society of men gathered around a teaching, round a person, round certain functions, of which some are lyrical—worship—or some are acts of God—sacraments—but which always belong to a human society directed Godward. This is a poor and insufficient vision of the Church. Looked at from this angle, the Church is nothing more than an object of historical study; it is not an object of faith, there is no invisible depth in that kind of vision of the Church. This presence of the invisible belongs to the Church because the first member of the Church is the Lord Jesus Christ who from two angles transcends the empirical, historical Church which we are, defined in the words, if you want, of St Ephraim of Syria, as not the assembly of the just, but the crowd of the sinners who repent and are seeking for eternal life. Christ transcends this empirical, historical, sociological group by the fact that as man in his very humanity, he is completely what we are, yet we doubt our brokenness, we doubt our separation from God, we doubt our separation from one another. Sin means basically separatedness, brokenness—inside, a sort of schizophrenia, outside, the fragmentation which we define when we see one another, not as parts, members, limbs of one body, but as individuals contrasted with us.

But also Christ transcends the sociological reality of the Church in another way. Even while He was within history in the days of His flesh, He belonged at the same time to the fullness of eternity because He is God, not only in his Godhead but because His humanity itself transforms life—finite, precarious, transitory as we know it—into life eternal, stable and victorious.

The Church is also the place where the Holy Spirit has taken abode, dwelling in each of us and making each of us a temple of the divine presence, and through the Holy Spirit we are united in one life, one reality, both physical and spiritual, with the Son of God, and we become, by participation, by adoption, the sons of the Father. The Church is an organism, both and equally human and divine, containing the fullness of God and the fullness of man, but also the frailty and brokenness and insufficiences of man, and in that sense the Church is simultaneously already at home and still in becoming—already at home in terms of relatedness to God by the way in which we are already grafted on God, and still in becoming because we have not reached the fullness to which we are going. In that sense, the Church also participates in this curious historicity and transcendence of Christ himself. Historical, yes, but bringing into history a dimension which is not to be imprisoned in time and space; the dimension of infinity, of eternity, of profundity, which *things* have not got apart from their participation in these qualities which are God Himself.

Now I want to turn to Christ, and to speak a little about his humanity. We read that He is truly man, and when we try to see what He has got in common with us, we see that He was born, He lived, He died. When we think of the way in which He participates in our life, we see he is not only a partaker of the glories of mankind—rather of anything but its glories. He makes himself solid, he identifies himself, not merely with those who are in glory, not merely with those who are just, righteous and saintly, not merely with those who are in no need of salvation or help—he identifies himself with everyone. We must not forget that the rich and the wealthy and the powerful also have an eternal soul, an eternal destiny; we must remember that to preach the Gospel to the poor and the derelict is only half of our mission. I am afraid the Church has forgotten that and for centuries has preached patience to one, hardly ever preaching justice to the other.

But it still remains that Christ, in his acceptance of the human situation, has identified himself with us, not only in our stability but also in our frailty and in our misery—yes, He hungered with us. He was born, rejected, there was no place for him except in a manger outside the society of man. He was surrounded with murder on the first day of His birth. He was tired, He was abandoned, lonely, hated, despised, and so forth; that is also true. He accepted the company of people whose company others didn't want—the sinners, those who were despised; that is also true. But there is something more to the way in which He accepts solidarity with us, and something much more important. He accepts solidarity with us *in death*. One says, quite naturally: he chose to become a man, so he had to die of it. No he hadn't, and this is just the point. A number of writers have pointed out the fact that death can be conceivable only through severance from the source of life. One cannot be, as it were, plugged into life eternal and die. St Maxim the Confessor underlines the fact that at the moment of his conception, at the moment of his birth, in his humanity Christ had no participation in death, because his humanity was pervaded with the eternal life of His divinity. He could not die. It is not an allegory or a metaphor when in the Orthodox Church on Thursday in Holy Week, we sing 'O Life Eternal, how can you die; O Light, how can you be quenched?'

This is a point which I think we should consider.

He died on the cross, and the operative words are the most tragic words of history: He, who is the Son of God, because he has accepted total, final, unreserved and unlimited solidarity with men in all their conditions, without participation in evil but accepting all its consequences; He, nailed on the cross, cries out the cry of forlorn humanity, 'My God, my God, why has thou forsaken me?'

People who are keen on exegesis explain to us that at that point He was rehearsing a verse of a prophetic song. If you have seen anyone die a violent death you can't well imagine him at the last moment rehearsing a prayer he had been taught when he was a little boy! Besides, it is an error of vision—for it is prophecy that is turned towards its fulfilment, not fulfilment that is supposed to recite words of prophecy. No, it was something real. When Christ said 'My God, my God why hast thou forsaken me', he was crying out, shouting out the words of a humanity that had lost God, and he was participating in that very thing which is the only real tragedy of humanity—all the rest is a consequence. The loss of God is death, is forlornness, is hunger, is separation. All the tragedy of man is in one word, 'Godlessness'. And He participates in our godlessness, not in the sense in which we reject God or do not know God, but in a more tragic way, in a way in which one can lose what is the dearest, the holiest, the most precious, the very heart of one's life and soul. And when in the Apostles' Creed, we repeat 'And he descended into Hell', we very often think 'That's one of those expressions', and we think of Dante and of the place where all those poor people are being tortured with such inventiveness by God.

But the Hell of the Old Testament has nothing to do with this spectacular hell of Christian literature. The Hell of the Old Testament is something infinitely more horrid; it is the place where God is not. It's the place of final dereliction, it's the place where you continue to exist and there is no life left. And when we say that He descended into Hell, we mean that having accepted the loss of God, to be one of us in the only major tragedy of that kind, He accepted also the consequences and goes to the place where God is not, to the place of final dereliction; and there, as ancient hymns put it, the Gates of Hell open to receive Him who was unconquered on earth and who now is conquered, a prisoner, and they receive this man who has accepted death in an immortal humanity, and Godlessness without sin, and they are confronted with the divine presence because he is both man and God, and Hell is destroyed—there is no place left where God is not. The old prophetic song is fulfilled, 'Where shall I flee from thy face—in Heaven is thy throne, in Hell (understand in Hebrew—the place where you are not), you are also'. This is the measure of Christ's solidarity with us, of his readiness to identify himself, not only with our misery but with our godlessness. If you think of that, you will realise that there is not one atheist on earth who has ever plunged into the depths of godlessness that the Son of God, become the Son of Man, has done. He is the only one who knows what it means to be without God and to die of it.

This has consequences in our attitude to people around us. If what I have been saying is true, and I believe it with all my commitment, then there is nothing which is human, including the loss of God, including death through loss of God, including all the anguish of the Garden of Gethsemane, which is the expectation of the coming of this horror of horrors, which is alien to Christ and which is outside the mystery of Christ.

And then what is our attitude as Christians to those who are the enemies of Christ, who hate him, who reject him and those who are Godless, not only because they have not yet met God, but because they have met a caricature of God, whom we have presented them with in the name of God Himself? We must realise that we stand before the judgement of those who reject

God because of us, and that Christ is not alien to them, and they are not outside Him, they are not alien to Him. There is a mystery of salvation far beyond the Church, far beyond our experience, far beyond our understanding.

What I have said about Christ is said not about the God of Heaven who becomes man, but about the Man, Jesus, who had such faith in us, in all of us, that he accepted becoming everything we are, including our Godlessness and our death. He believed in us and was prepared to vindicate the greatness of man by showing us in his person that man is so great that when God unites Himself with him, man remains in the full sense of the word—only instead of remaining small, he becomes what God has willed him to be.

ONE EXPRESSION dominated the Oxford University Mission in 1969 which is particularly clear to Ian Ramsey, the Bishop of Durham. Many could not immediately understand what it meant, but then discovered that it had a depth of meaning and it served a very useful purpose. The expression of 'cosmic disclosure'. Cosmic disclosure means to him and came to mean generally that there are moments when things which surround us—people, situations—suddenly acquire depth, become transparent, as it were, and allow us to see them with a new significance, and as I said, with depth. The nearest approximation to cosmic disclosure I could give you is something which we probably all know about. When I was small I was given a little drawing made up of a maze of lines. What you could distinguish at once in this maze of lines was a hunter in a wood, and the caption said 'Where is the rabbit?' Then you took the thing and began to look at it this way and that way in all directions, until suddenly you saw the rabbit and you couldn't understand how it was that you hadn't seen it before.

That is true as an image for everything in life. We live in a situation, live with people, see the situation at its face value, we see people apparently as they are, and one day we suddenly spot the goodness. How great, how profoundly significant that is. That happens, for instance, when we look at very familiar scenery one day when we are perceptive, when we have eyes to see, and are capable of response. We look at something which is the most ordinary thing which we have seen day after day, and suddenly we stand arrested by beauty, by meaning, by something it lends us, as though things had become translucent and we could see in depth, deeper and deeper towards a core that is full of meaning.

The same happens with people. We live among people and we see them as people. People are interchangeable with the crowd, faces move and there is always a face to be seen. But all of a sudden a face that we have seen often, which has become so familiar that we don't even look at it any more because from the first glimpse we know that's him or that's her—suddenly we have stopped to look, or because something in the eyes, something in the expression has made us stop, the face appears to us completely new, lending us a depth of meaning, a depth of significance. And someone who was an interchangeable part of the crowd is singled out in such a way that it becomes a person, and a person who is totally unique, who can't be replaced by any other person, can't be confused, is simply himself or herself.

There is a saying of Methodius Olympius, a Greek divine, who said 'As long as we don't love a person, one person, we are surrounded with men and women. The moment our heart has discovered the person it loves there is the beloved one and nothing but people around.' This is the way in which something can be singled out, seen in depth and in truth—seen, I was about to say, in glory, because in those moments things which are lifeless, colourless or dull, suddenly acquire relief, colour, beauty and meaning. In such moments occurs what Ian Ramsey, the Bishop of Durham, calls 'cosmic disclosure'. That kind of cosmic disclosure we all know, and if we are attentive to ourselves we will remember such moments—moments when suddenly, among people whom we know very well, we discover someone, with a warmth of heart, with a vision, with an emotion we never had before. A thought that has been repeatedly thrust at us in the form of quotation from the Gospel or from literature, which somehow clicks in a situation and acquires deep meaning, is no longer a quotation from Shakespeare or from the Scriptures; it is truth that has been put into words which are so significant and so powerful.

This kind of experience adjoins the experience which we have of God because God is also someone whom we can discover in this experience of cosmic disclosure. I insist on the word 'cosmic' this time because God is within the reality in which we live, and furthermore, as long as we have not discovered Him and the invisible world that is His world, we are still blind to a whole wealth of reality. This is why it is important, from my point of view, to have discovered God. In a way I would say it is rather a danger, very often a nuisance. One could very well live with less trouble without a God than with a God because— particularly with a God who has accepted solidarity to the point of death, love to the point of forgetting himself and in addition to this, is vulnerable, helpless, despised, beaten—God tells us coldbloodedly; this is the example which I give you—follow it. Or he says, here are the beatitudes: you will be hungry, you will be thirsty, you will be beaten, you will be cast out, you will be persecuted—and that is the best you can have. That kind of God is not always a discovery that brings ease in our lives. The point is not whether God will be useful, the point is whether it is true that He exists.

Now, can one attach any truth, any validity, to this kind of cosmic disclosure which includes beauty, love, human relationships, the existence of God, and a new vision of the world? What is the validity of experience? There is a point of view which I believe to be a falsification of a scientific approach that says: experience is something that can be proved according to methods of natural science or the precise sciences like physics, chemistry, biology. This, I think, is a falsification because experience is not limited to that kind of science. There is a whole world which is irrational, yet not unreasonable. When I was a student and studied physics, I had to pass the exam on acoustics. I was totally uninterested in music and totally incapable of appreciating it at all. To me, music was a system of sounds. I knew all about music as far as sound is concerned and as far as physics is involved; as to enjoying it—no, it never occurred to me that it was enjoyable. I had also met a man who took the same line about literature— a very remarkable man I met in Ireland, an old canon who was the shyest and the most reserved creature I have ever met and

who found the English extraordinary, and so unbearably
exuberant that he could not stand a holiday in Britain because
he came back exhausted. He asked me once whether I knew
Dostoevsky. I was rather surprised that he was interested in
Dostoevsky and I said, 'Have you read him? How do you like
his novels?' He looked at me and said, 'Novels? I never thought
he wrote novels'. I said, 'What did you read then?' He
mentioned all Dostoevsky's well-known books. I asked 'What
were you looking for?' It turned out that he was collecting a
card index on Russian religion and he had read the whole of
Dostoevsky but had never noticed that he was a writer.

There is such a thing as the irrational that cannot be simply
reduced to rational formulae. We know now that there is a whole
world of the irrational in us which is not in the realm of intellect
and reason, yet which exists and has immense power in us.
Emotional troubles are not rational and yet they are more
decisive in our total balance than our points of view, when in
an Olympian way, that is, with total indifference, we view
things. But there is another thing about the kind of experience
which people would advocate, saying 'That is reliable, I have
probed into it with my five senses?' But our five senses are no
more reliable than any kind of inner reaction. When you look at
something, you say: I am sure it is there; my eyes give me
evidence. When I listen to something, I say: I am sure it is there;
my ears have given me evidence. But what is the evidence? I
remember very well, I went to see a patient once, who sat next
to me and as I was talking to her she suddenly began to pat thin
air. I said 'Oh, what's that?' And the good lady said, 'It's an
ethereal lion. I live in an astral body and not only in a physical
body, and I have a nice little lion that comes and sits with me'.
This good lady felt the lion's fur under her hand; she could see
the lion; she could probably perceive the lion in a variety of
other ways. I couldn't I'm afraid. Now, from my point of view
her physical perception of the lion was hallucinatory; from her
point of view the reason for my lack of perception was my dense-
ness and my blindness. With everything we see, we assume first
of all that previous experience is proof that it is true, and secondly
we pass a judgement of value, that this is not a hallucination and

that it is reality. From the point of view of natural life, of course we may be right or wrong, but from the point of view of psychological thinking, I have a right to challenge and to doubt any visual, audible, sensory experience because your eyes are not the part of you that assert that this is a lion or that this is a watch. It is your judgement and your head, your brains that say that. And between the lion that sits here and your eyes that catch sight of him in his absence and the nervous system that brings it to your brain and your brain that takes cognisance of it and your judgement that says it is a real lion and not a fantasy is a nice long chain which I can doubt at more than one point.

One can show experimentally that many of the things which we assume so easily are more doubtful than we imagine. So that unless we are prepared, as philosophers or scientists have been to doubt systematically any experience we have, there is no logical, solid reason to question one type of experience and admit of the other, especially when a type of experience is not the experience of one unique person, but when it is corroborated by the experience, the practical knowledge of other people.

So the fact that an experience will not be transmitted directly or cannot be given evidence of by what we call objective methods is proof of nothing, because the words objective and subjective must be treated with a great deal more care. An objective judgement usually means a judgement which I can pass with total indifference, without any kind of prejudice, and in practice that's what we mean by this. But if we want to have an objective vision of something, what we should really mean by this is that we must perceive the thing as the thing perceives itself without interfering. That is obviously totally impossible; I cannot perceive a chair by identifying myself with the chair. But I do perceive something when something happens to me. So long as it remains only the object and unrelated to me, there is no perception at all, not to speak of any kind of experience. I think we must take that into account, because neither in music, nor in physics, nor in any kind of rational and precise science, is there objectivity that does not involve a subject. And if that is true, then all the complex experiences of beauty, of love, of appreciation, of evaluation of judgement, of inner certainty which we can have, have an objective significance for another person.

Now, this is an important introduction because unless we understand this, we have got to deny systematically any experience which is not tangible and we can doubt any experience which is tangible unless we accept a total interplay of immutable laws of identity in the outside world and in the laws of nature.

There is another problem. In this intercourse between subjective and objective, there are two things. First of all, an experience which has become mine, I must be able to retain, to examine and to express; and on the other hand, the people around me must be able to receive the experience, that is, to receive the message of it. There is more than one way of conveying an experience, but the most usual is by forms of speech that are meaningful simultaneously on two levels—on the level of the objective experience which you have had, but also on the level of something already known to the listener than can work as an analogy and enable him to understand what you are speaking about. So, when we speak of love, there is the love of the mother to the child, the love of the child to the mother; they are not identical. The love of friends, the mutual love of lovers; the love of husband and wife, and a variety of lofty types of love are very different from one another because you cannot understand it before you have undergone it. A little girl of seven will never be able to understand what it means that her sister of eighteen is madly in love, because there is an analogy but not yet identity between the two. So there are ways of conveying things.—

Take a man like Jeremiah. Jeremiah was shown by God, one day, a twig of almond tree, and God spoke to him at the same time and said, 'What do you see?' The answer was 'God is the keeper of Israel.' This is built on a grammatical pun in the Hebrew language which is irrelevant for what we need now. But can you imagine the state in which Jeremiah was; he saw the twig of almond tree and all of a sudden he was overwhelmed with the sense of the divine presence. Don't you think that whenever he held in his hand a twig of almond tree, he was brought back to that much more than by a sort of theological reminiscence? Don't you know what happens to you when you have been in a place where you have been miserable or happy and come back after ten years, and suddenly see the same sunlight, the same house, the same situation, how, of a sudden, all the emotions of ten years ago well up in you which you could not conjure up by any trick of intellectual imagination?

This is the first way in which any experience which was reality has become now my own past, has placed myself in the position which I defined in the first chapter as the point where certainty about something which has become visible to me at a certain moment can be retained. And then perhaps I will want to convey something about it. Then I will use words that are either words of poetry or methods of music, something that will make sense to my listener because he may have an analogical experience and be able to catch a glimpse of mine through the glimpse of his. That is what happens, for instance, to us when we have endured real suffering or enjoyed exhilerating happiness. We can understand the joy and the suffering of others, not by suffering their suffering or rejoicing with their joy, but by compassion, suffering together, or rejoicing together, with them, with understanding.

The seers, the visionaries, the people who have the experience of things invisible that they have undergone as certainties, try to express things. They usually use words that are ordinary words to convey an experience that would make sense.

Take, for instance, the old man Nicodemus, who came to see the Lord one night at Jerusalem. You can imagine the scene. They stood probably on the platform of the house to talk in the evening breeze instead of staying in the heated rooms. They were speaking of God, intangible, invisible, that cannot be caught in any kind of net. Nicodemus didn't understand, and Christ said 'Look, what do you perceive now? You perceive the wind that is blowing around us; your skin is refreshed, your clothes are freely moving in this wind. It is an actuality, a certainty that you are within this refreshing, life-giving, renewing blowing of the evening breeze. Yet, you don't know where it comes from, you don't know where it goes to. You know nothing about it except this complete personal experience that makes you say an objective thing: "The wind is blowing, I am refreshed".'

The Church in the Scriptures has been spoken of as being the Bride of the Lamb. I remember talking in those terms once in a youth group led by a very pious and dignified lady. When question time came, she said 'I can't understand, why do you and your Church use all these fairy tale expressions? What do they convey?' I thought that they did convey something, but the group wanted to know why. So I said 'Does "Bride of the Lamb" convey anything to you about the Church?' She replied 'It's ridiculous, I know what a lamb is; we have all seen Easter postcards, the little white beast with a blue or red ribbon jumping on the green meadow; and we also know what a bride is, it's a girl who has realised that it's time to get married and looks round for a boy to catch who has got a good job, a car and a future.' Now, this respectable Christian lady obviously could not see the point that the bride is a girl who proves capable and ready to love with such commitment, to love so wholeheartedly, as to choose one man, to unite her destiny with him, to be prepared to abandon all the rest, to follow him wherever he will go. And if you remember what Scripture called the lamb in the 52nd/53rd chapter of Isaiah, you will understand what the man of sorrows and the lamb means. Then yes, the Church is expressed by these terms. But at that point, it is human experience plus a depth of communal experience that is needed. Outside the communal experience and the vocabulary of a legal community, these words mean nothing any more.

Among the ways in which we express our knowledge of things invisible and of God in particular, there are words which try to qualify God—either in his relatedness to us, as the Creator, or in his actions within our life of freedom—or else point to something which is at the very core of the problem. And there are three such words: the one is *God*—God is a very fortunate word because it means nothing semantically. I don't mean to say that a philologist doesn't know where its roots begin; what I mean is that when you say 'God', the word itself hasn't got any content—it signifies someone or a notion, but it doesn't describe him. So that we can speak this word without prejudging anything. And there are two more words: *Jesus* and *Love*; the two ways in which we know God. In the word *Jesus*, we say 'Who is God?'

God is this man who claims to be the Eternal One, Jesus, who is God and is man at the same time; to whom I can speak personally and who reveals to me therefore that God is a person because only a person can become one with a person, and reveal a person. And on the other hand Love. Love which is not simply in Biblical terminology a feeling multiplied by infinity, but is the fullness of life that is beyond insecurity, has conquered death, and can give itself as an offering of life and death without fear.

I have already said all I wanted to say about the way in which Jesus of Nazareth, who belonged totally to history and at the same time transcends history completely in his Godhead, is involved and totally involved in our human destiny. But what I want to talk about is the fact that we do not only say that the Son of God became the Son of Man; we say, we proclaim, we believe, we see that God became flesh, the Word became flesh, and by flesh I indicate the fact that God became not only part of history or destiny, but of the material, visible, tangible reality of this world. Matter has found itself in the fact of the incarnation, united with divinity. What I have said earlier about man holds here. The incarnation reveals to us that man is so great that he can unite himself with God without ceasing to be man in the full sense of this word; that he is so vast that he contains the divine presence, that there is at the core of each of us what the Archbishop of Canterbury once called a God-shaped emptiness which nothing can fill which is of the earth or of heaven or of the created, but God alone. But here we see the greatness, not only of humanity, but of the material world revealed to us in the historical fact of the incarnation. If God has taken flesh, it means that in an exemplary manner in the human flesh of the man called Jesus, all the matter of this world has been shown to be capable of such vastness, such depth, such greatness as to be united with the Godhead without ceasing to be itself, but becoming to a degree and in a way which surpasses imagination itself in the full sense of this word. So we discover that matter— which we treat usually in almost a sacrilegious way as inert, dead, alien to the great calling of the creation—can become not only spirit-bearing, but God-bearing, pervaded with divinity. And this we can see in the way in which matter is revealed in the miracle of the transfiguration. We do not see light divine shine around Christ, we see his flesh aflame with divine light; we see his clothes become whiter than they can be made on earth; we can see that matter itself is pervaded, filled with the divine presence, and revealed in glory for however short a moment.

That is the background for the root of our belief and for our faith in a realistic theology of the sacraments and for a realistic vision of miracles. Miracles are usually thought of in a most primitive way by the least primitive people. People imagine that they are so sophisticated that they have outgrown the very notion of matter, forgetting that they eat every day, they multiply, they take baths; that they are the victims, fearful and careful of every change of temperature. What I mean by a miracle is not something which strikes the imagination because it couldn't happen and yet it does happen. The difference between a miracle and an act of magic is that an act of magic consists of an act of over-powering, of enslaving, of depriving someone of something—of freedom, of independence, of the capability to determine itself and to stand in its own right.

A miracle is, on the contrary, an act of God which is mediated by the faith of man and the divine mercy that re-establishes a harmony, destroyed and broken. And at the root of it there is this very clear vision of the Old and the New Testaments, that all things created by God are created for eternity, for destiny, created capable of hearing God, of understanding God, of obeying God in a fulfilment which is both freedom and obedience. That applies also to the sacraments in a peculiar way. In the sacraments what we believe happens is that the matter of this world is detached from the evil, sinful, Godless context in which it was betrayed by the faithlessness of men, brought back to God as an offering, received by God, made free, restored to its primeval freshness, and furthermore by an act divine, fulfilled and revealed as it should be and shall be. To take the central act of the Church, the blessing of the bread and the wine into the body and the blood of Christ—it ultimately means that we see here the matter of this world in the example of a small particle of it, of a drop of it, attain to that fulfilment which is the vocation of all things, that God should be all in all and that all things should be fulfilled by the divine presence, indeed the integration of God in them.

That is the meaning of *Jesus*, which implies incarnation, history and the taking up of flesh by the living God; it implies a personal relationship which opens up our vision of men, of all things created; and it implies that the scientist, the physician, anyone who deals with the matter of this world, is a high priest or else has betrayed his human vocation and in particular his Christian vocation.

The other word I have mentioned is Love. We read in the Scriptures that God is Love. We read also in the Scriptures, in a synthetic way by bringing together things which are not expressed as a theological statement, that God is one in the Holy Trinity. The two things are identical. I want in a few words to say something about love, then to try to show the relation of this notion of love to the Holy Trinity—One God.

We usually think of love in terms of taking of love, of giving and of receiving; and this is right. But, first of all, giving and receiving is not what we understand by it. It must be something much deeper and purer, more refined than what we imagine we do when we give and when we receive. Very often to give is a way we have of asserting ourselves. We are rich and therefore we are secure, and the proof of our security is that we can give. We are proud and generous as a result and we revel in the sense of our generosity and greatness because it gives us the right to be proud. When we are at the receiving end at times, we can receive because we are greedy. But these two actions of giving and receiving must, to become Christian actions, be free from the evils I have indicated. You cannot receive with an open heart, with a sense of worshipful gratitude, with a sense of joy or fulfilment, of exhilarating openness unless you love the person who gives, and unless you know the gift is a sign of love and has nothing to do with pride and self-assertiveness. You cannot give in the right way if giving is not committing yourself to the last and is not an expression of service, of worship, and of tenderness. And this is one aspect of love.

But love is not only this. St Gregory of Nazianzus in the 4th century, speaking of God, trying to find the link between love

and the Trinity makes an analysis of human love to try to find
the clue, because if we are using human words, human images,
it is legitimate also to see connections on the human level. He
says love that would be simply an arithmetical one, a monad
cannot be called love. It is self-love, self-adoration, narcissism.
He turns to the love of two and says, 'People imagine that the
love of two, of a couple, that know nothing any more except the
two who love one another, is fullness of love. Don't we see the
passion, the total commitment, the adoration, indeed, which
results from it?' And he says 'No, this is a fallacy, because this
love is frail. However rich and however pure the giving and
receiving between these persons, this relationship is not stable.'
The whole of literature, and unfortunately so much in our lives,
proves that the moment a third person appears, we are either in
comedy or in tragedy. It is either Othello or any other example
of the betrayed husband or wife. It is either tragic and ends in
death and murder, or else it ends in the laughter of the
onlookers. What happens is that this double link, this two-way
traffic of giving and receiving, breaks down if it is not an open
relationship, if it is a closed circuit that goes round and round.
When the third person appears, a triangular relationship is established in which giving and receiving can be pictured now in the
form of two arrows which meet each other or are directed against
each other. And a new system of relationship is established—the
newcomer establishes a golden link of adulterous love with the
one, and a bloody link of hatred with the other; it is a triangle
of complex relationships, it is not an image of love.

What Gregory of Nazianzus insists on is that love implies
a third quality—not only giving and receiving, but the ability
of sacrifice. Now, the word sacrifice in our language means always
losing something, being deprived of something. But in Latin, in
Greek, in Hebrew, in Slavonic, in all the ancient languages,
sacrifice comes from sacred—it means to make something sacred,
make something holy and not to lose it. Indeed, when you bring
life to God or a gift to God, it becomes His, it is no longer yours
in the greedy and possessive sense of the word. But it becomes
holy with the holiness of God, and we must remember that when
we speak of sacrifice, it is that which is the centre of gravity—

not what you lose, but what happens when we bring the bread and the wine, the holy and perfect sacrifice. What happens is sanctification and not simply loss, because there is no loss when we bring something to God—what we have we receive from God, more than we could provide ourselves with. 'Seek the Kingdom of God', says Christ, 'and all things will be given to you in addition', not: 'taken away from you'. This is the principle of sacrifice, of santification, of the offering that gives and receives only as an act of love and not to gain a return.

The word which I would use is self-annihilation, the ability to accept not to be, no longer to exist in a situation because something else matters more. By this I mean the following: John the Baptist said about himself, 'I am the friend of the Bridegroom'. The bride is not his bride, neither is the bridegroom his bridegroom, but such is his love for both of them that he brings them together—he is their witness and their companion in the marriage feast; he brings them to the chamber where they will meet face to face alone in a fulfilled relationship of soul and body, and he remains outside lying across the door so that no one should disturb the mystery of this love.

This act of self-annihilation is essential to love, and if there is no such thing in our love with regard not only to one person but to all persons, all situations, all things, our love is still deficient. This is very important for us to understand because in God we find the three things. We find the exulting joy of three persons who love in giving perfectly and receiving perfectly, but who being a trinitarian relationship, if I may put it in this form of speech, are not in the way of each other, in which each of them accepts every single moment not to exist for the two others to be face to face—the miracle of total communion, fusion and oneness.

Speaking of God we must consider things in the simultaneity of events and not in temporal succession. The three simultaneously give, the three simultaneously receive, the three simultaneously place themselves in such a situation that the others are alone with each other. But that means death because self-annihilation, self-nothing, sacrifice, mean death and the cross is inscribed in the mystery of the Holy Trinity.

We speak of the impassibility of God. So often the impassibility of God is understood as the inability of God to feel anything. The word doesn't mean that at all; it means simply that God is never acted upon, is never passive, is always supremely active. The incarnation and the death upon the cross, unless the cross was inscribed in the very mystery of the trinitarian life, would be an event introduced into God from the outside. In fact, on the contrary, it is the projection of one of the rich aspects of a complex mystery of love into human history through the incarnation and the death, because it is always there as the death of the one who accepts not being in order that the others may be fulfilled. But then you will say, 'Is there only death within this mystery? Is it only death which we can expect from each other if we love in a more perfect way?'

Indeed not, because there is something else to it. There is a saying of Gabriel Marcel which I feel is one of the great statements of Christian thought in our days. He says 'To tell someone "I love you" is tantamount to telling him or her, "you shall never die" '. We usually try to assert our existence, to be sure that we are, to conquer our insecurity, our doubt. We assert ourselves against. We distinguish one another by putting together common qualities of size, colour, language and so on, that allow us to say, 'He is not me'. But this is the state of the individual, and the individual is a state of fragmentation.

This is not what is the object and subject of love. It is the person that is the identity in us which makes us the same person from the baby to the old man, and from earth into heaven. This person cannot contrast himself or herself by opposition because it is uniqueness that is characteristic. But then, if you accept dying as an individual, dying as someone who tries to assert his being by not being the other, how can you survive? Only in the love of the other. And this is Trinitarian theology—the vision of three persons whose love is such that they lay down their lives and they are caught up into eternal life, into life that can no longer be taken away from them because they have given their lives and others have granted them eternity.

This is an anthropomorphic way of speaking of the Trinity, you will say. Yes it is, but the revelation of God is always in human terms because it is addressed to human beings; whatever can be revealed by God about Himself can be revealed only if there is a conformity between the object who is revealed to and the subject who reveals it. All that can be revealed must be capable of being put in human terms. What we forget and where we make our God extraordinarily small, and indeed not acceptable for many Christians and non-Christians is that we imagine God is nothing but what can be revealed about him.

Between husband and wife there is a transcendence of two persons into something greater. A German writer has put it in the following way: 'In marriage two become one in such a way that it is one personality in two persons,' and beyond that there is all the mystery of God which is beyond communicating, which is beyond being shared with us, which is Him unbelievable. In that way then we will see that God is infinitely vaster than the model and image that we have, but all these models and images belong also to the mystery of revelation. A God like Him is, on all these levels, to us a revelation of transcendence and at the same time, of humanity. He is as great as man is, and we are as great as He is. He belongs to our becoming and our tragedy, totally, and we belong to the fullness of his ability and glory, wholly by vocation, and yet, not in possession of it because we are still on the way.

If we think in that context about man and history and individual persons, about matter and science and technology, about human soul and human art, then we can have a vision of the cosmos and of the God who is within it and beyond it, that can inspire us to be creative, as creative as God, and, at the same time, to worship Him in amazement because we have been given this incredible freedom to be ourselves.

CHAPTER FOUR

HOLINESS AND PRAYER[1]

I T is very important for the comprehension of holiness to understand that it has two poles: *God* and the *World*. Its source, its fulcrum and its content is God; but its point of impact, the place into which it is born, where it develops and also where it is expressed in terms of Christ's salvation, is the world, this ambiguous world which, on the one hand, was created by God and is the object of such love that the Father gave His only-begotten Son for its salvation, and on the other hand, has fallen into the slavery of evil. This pole of holiness which relates to the world therefore has two aspects: a vision of the world as God willed it, as He loves it, and at the same time an asceticism which requires us to disengage ourselves from the world and free the world from the grip of Satan.

This second element, this battle which is our vocation, is part and parcel of holiness. The Desert Fathers, the ascetics of early times, did not flee from the world in the sense in which modern man sometimes tries to escape its grip in order to find a haven of security, they set out to conquer the Enemy in battle. By the grace of God, in the power of the Spirit, they were engaging in combat.

One of the reasons why holiness is unsteady and why the holiness of the Fathers and heroes of the Spirit in the early days often seems so remote is that we have lost this sense of combat. The conception of the Church as the advance guard of the Kingdom, as men and women who have committed their ultimate weakness into God's hands, knowing with certainty that the very

[1] A talk given in Louvain in 1969.

power of God is able to manifest itself in their weakness, the conception of the Church as the Body of Christ, whose life is not taken from it but which gives its life, is a rare thing among Christians. More often we see that as soon as a community or an individual is confronted with danger, he turns to the Lord and says: 'Lord, help me, protect me, save me, deliver me!' Isn't this the picture which the Polish writer Sinkiewicz gave us years ago in *'Quo Vadis'* in which St Peter leaves Rome at the moment of persecution and at the gates of the city meets Christ who is on His way there. 'Where are you going, Lord?' he asks his Master. 'I am going back to Rome,' the Lord replies, 'to suffer and die there because you are leaving it.' Isn't this what we constantly expect of God? Isn't this our anguished, desperate appeal to the Lord as soon as life becomes dangerous: 'Deliver me, Lord!' When the psalmist spoke of this deliverance, his position was quite different from ours; he belonged to the Old Testament. We belong to the New Testament, we are the Body of Christ, the temple of the Holy Spirit. God has sent us into the world by His Son, just as He sent His Son into the world.

And so in this respect there is a *crisis of holiness* which does not date from our time, for it is contemporaneous with many Christian generations. But we must face it, because holiness is our absolute vocation, because contemplative holiness is not an escape, and because the activism of our time which tries to be independent of any contemplation and to become a value in itself, lacks the content of complete holiness which Christian holiness ought to have, for the content of holiness is God Himself.

If you would like to make a closer study of holiness from the point of view of the Old Testament, you can easily refer to the alphabetical index of the Jerusalem Bible. There you will find all the elements that have been considered since before Christ. I would like to single out one or two without dealing with the subject as a whole.

God alone is holy. To say that God is holy is not to define Him as having holiness as an attribute, because we do not know this attribute. In saying 'God is holy', we do not define Him, because holiness itself is unknown to us: it becomes perceptible to us in proportion to our discovering God. For Israel holiness was that which is God. Reverential fear was linked to this notion; likewise the sense of irremediable separation: God is transcendent in an absolute way, He is beyond everything. Even when God is known, He remains unknowable; even when He approaches, He remains infinitely far away; even when He speaks to us, He is still beyond all communication. To approach Him is a danger: He is the fire that consumes; one cannot see His face and remain alive. All these images show us the attitude of a people who were conscious of the holiness of God and who were face to face with this Living God.

But the scandal of the New Testament, the impossible thing, is that the Inaccessible One has become accessible, the transcendent God has become flesh and dwelt among us. The holiness which surpassed every human notion and was a separation reveals itself to be otherwise: the very holiness of God can become infinitely close without becoming any the less mysterious; it becomes accessible without our being able to possess it; it lays hold of us without destroying us. In this perspective we can understand the words of St Peter in his general epistle, that we are called to become partakers of the divine nature. In Christ we see something which could be revealed by God but which could not even be dreamed of by man: the fullness of Divinity in human flesh. Here is the crux of holiness. It is accessible to us because of the fact of the Incarnation. This does not lessen the mystery of God: a purely transcendent God is easier to understand or imagine than the God of the Incarnation. And when we see the crèche of the Nativity in our imagination or in plastic representations and can take the Child-God in our hands, we are confronted with a greater mystery than that of the imperceptible God. How can we understand that the full depth of infinity and eternity lies here, hidden and at the same time revealed by a frail human body that is fragile and transparent to the presence of God?

Here is the very crux of holiness, because our holiness can be nothing else than participation in the holiness of God. And this is possible only through Christ, although the Old Testament was aware of a created holiness within the created world. Everything which God lays hold of and which becomes His own possession, such as the Ark, a person, a holy place, participates in a certain way in God's holiness and becomes an object of reverential fear. There is a holiness of Presence: the Temple. There is a holiness disquieting for the neighbouring peoples: the People of God, who are the place of the Presence. But this place of the Presence, which was like a living Temple, does not participate in God's holiness in a personal way, in each of its members. It is only later, in the Church of the Living God, that the place of the Presence also becomes the place of a personal presence within and through each one: it is the Church, the Body of Christ, the Church which Christ is on the evening of His Resurrection, in the Holy Spirit who takes hold of the Church, brings it to birth and becomes its life; but it is also the Church each of whose members, on the day of Pentecost and through the centuries by a continuation of that mystery, become the temple of the living God. And the Church is not only linked to Christ as His Body and to the Spirit, whose temple she becomes, but it is a Church in which each member in his particular uniqueness is linked to the Father through the only-begotten Son. 'Your life', says St Paul, 'is hidden in God with Christ.' This relationship of Christ with us, this bond between the One who alone is holy and His creatures, this presence of the personal eternity and personal infinity that God is, this real and living participation in a divine holiness is the essential characteristic of the Church, or at least one of its central characteristics. I believe that the Church is holy, not simply blessed and sanctified by gifts of grace, but holy with a depth and intensity which surpass all meaure, holy with the holiness of God who resides there, in the way in which a piece of wood glows with the fire that consumes it. And this holiness is a Presence in the Church. This is why the Church, in its position in relation to God, can acquire, possess and live this holiness only in Him.

On the other hand, just as God became man, just as His holiness was present in the flesh in our midst, living, acting and saving, so too now, through the mystery of the Incarnation, the Church participates in eternity, in the holiness of God, and at the same time also in the salvation of the world. The holiness of the Church must find its place in the world in an act of crucified love, in an active and living presence. But essentially it is the holiness, the Presence of God that we should manifest in the world. This is our vocation, this is what we are. If we are not this, we are outside the mystery that we pretend to express and in which we pretend to have our part.

Nevertheless, it is necessary to locate the position of the Church and that of the individual Christian in relation to the world. It seems to me that we have only two ways of doing this: on the one hand, we can try to see what holiness has been in history, and on the other hand, we can try to understand, in the person of Christ and in divine love, what the world is for God and what the solidarity of God is with the world that He has created.

I believe that a careful study of the history of the saints will easily show us that throughout the ages holiness has been the expression of love. In the very brief and condensed history of the Russian Church—it is hardly a thousand years since we became Christians—we can see something extremely important: the forms of saintliness have changed through the centuries without disappearing once they have come into being, and these changes express through the years the way in which God, in the hearts of the faithful, have loved the world. Scanning the history of the Russian Church—the one I know best—I see that at the beginning there is an act of faith: a man or a human group who believed, and who gave God to the surrounding people. St Vladimir, Prince of Kiev, believed. And because he believed passionately, radically, Christ entered into the history of his principality, and the social and human structures began to break up and be transformed. Yet he had no social purpose, no pious work in view: he simply could not live otherwise than he had learned from God Himself. It is only because this man believed in the Gospel message that the relations and internal structures in his principality changed. It is curious to note this change during a period when there was certainly no talk of social security or of a state responsible for its citizens! We see in the first place that this man, who had been a man of war and violence, a powerful and authoritarian tribal chief, ceased to make war, opened the prisons and proclaimed the forgiveness of Christ. We see that this man, whose personal life was by no means a model of holiness, changed overnight with a sharpness and clarity which confronted his people with a choice: to follow the old vision or a new one. We see that in the structures of this poor little city of Kiev, which was no more than a market-town, the poor, the sick and the aged became the object of solicitude. All the poor who could still walk received their daily meal in the courtyards of the Prince's palace. For those who were too aged, too weak, unable to move about, the Prince sent carts loaded with bread and sustenance through the city and neighbouring hamlets. Here we have a picture of a social transformation as great, comparatively speaking, as the greatest of our time. It implies a change of mental habit more amazing than the improvements that we make from day to day within one mentality already acquired and given to us.

This is the first picture: living, active love, the diaconate of Christ.

Then, a little later, we have the witness of the martyr, a particular type of martyr. There is no doubt that the Russian Church, like all the others, has known martyrs for the faith: people who set out to preach the Gospel to tribes that were still pagans perished for their message. Among them are two men who expressed a type of holiness that we would call 'social'. They were two princes, Boris and Gleb—and even a third, Igor —who chose to give up their power and principality and their very life rather than draw the sword. They allowed themselves to be killed rather than be defended and cause bloodshed. Here again is an example of holiness contemporaneous with an era of violence, one in which violence breaks out in new forms and in a new situation. Here again we see that the Gospel creates a situation of love, and that it is love alone which defines holiness in this situation.

Then a dark age: Russia is invaded for three centuries and falls under the Mongol yoke. At this time we find only two types of holiness, that of bishops and that of princes, both of which express the same thing. Their holiness arises out of the fact that both are hard pressed, being the defenders, advocates and protectors of the people committed to their charge, and they give their life, their blood, for the people. At this moment all the other forms of holiness that have existed—monastic holiness and others—become sporadic. Then a veritable epidemic of holiness begins: that of people who give their lives for their neighbour, truly taking responsibility for him according to the image of Kings and Priests which the Old Testament gives us. They realise that sometimes, in so-called 'better' times, the heads of the Church as well as those of the state forget that they stand on the threshold of two worlds: the world of men and the world of God; the world of the unique, radiant divine will directed to the salvation and plenitude of all things, and the world of multiple, discordant, violent human will opposed to that of God,—and that their role is to unite the two and to give their life for this work. Here again we see that it is love that takes the lead.

It is not a new invention in terms of holiness, it is not the search for a contemporary holiness: it is simply the response of the holiness inherent in the Church, of the love given by God to His Church, which has found a new form of expression. It was not the moment to withdraw into the forests or to choose other valid but different forms of holiness: it was the moment for giving one's life.

The Mongol yoke withdraws: we enter a period of national anguish, a period in which the former suffering now changes to confidence. As long as this suffering was crushing the nation and destroying the very capacity to feel it, it was bearable. Now problems arise, internal ones which are not yet well expressed: God and suffering, the horror of a world which could be so frightful, and then the birth of hope and the search for a path for this hope. At this time we see giants of the spiritual life one after the other abandoning everything, the highest tasks as well as the humblest circumstances, and withdrawing into the forests of northern and central Russia to seek God there. These men leave everything because they have understood that in torment, disorder and purely earthly seeking they will not find the answer to the problems of their contemporaries. They leave everything to be with God. Their purpose is certainly not social at this time. They have to find their souls again, and with their soul, the nation, the soul of their people, the soul of their contemporaries. They are not in flight: they take up a life so arduous, so laborious that it would be ridiculous to consider it as an escape. The living conditions in a forest in northern Russia at this time, the hunger, cold, physical dangers from wild beasts, all these should make it easy for us to understand that it is not an easy and comfortable life that they are looking for. They seek only God, and they find God in the depths of their souls, which surrender to Him. They seek only Him, but at the same time their love becomes deeper and deeper, and they welcome all those who, one after the other, come in the same anguish, seeking the same haven of salvation. Monasteries grow up around them, this too by an act of love. A society of human help and work begins to appear. I will give two examples that are diametrically opposed.

In norther Russia beyond the Volga in the 15th century one of the great saints of Russia, St Nilus, settled with several companions in a desolate, swampy region. They lived in dreadful poverty, and in his *Rule* St Nilus said that a monk must be so poor that he cannot even offer physical charity beyond a piece of bread, but he should love the pilgrim or the vagabond or the brigand who has fled or the heretic who has broken away from the Church—let us say, the Church that St Nilus belongs to— he should love him so much that he would be ready to give him all the spiritual experience, everything that his soul contained. Here is a man who chose to know only Christ, and Christ crucified, who gave up everything, physically, and who could not give anything, for he possessed nothing but God alone, by whom he was possessed. For one does not possess God: one is laid hold of by Him, filled with His breath and His presence, but one does not become the proprietor of all this.

The other man, his contemporary, lived in the region of Moscow and was an equally remarkable person. He founded a monastery in which about a thousand monks worked under a rule of incredible austerity. The monastery, in such a cold region, was never heated, the monks were not permitted to wear anything else but a hair shirt and a garment thrown over it. The offices lasted ten hours a day and the work in the fields or in the monastery was seven to eight hours. At times they groan and howl with indignation, saying, 'We are hungry, our granaries are full . . . and you do not let us eat; we are thirsty and we have water . . . and you do not let us drink.' Their holy and fierce superior answers: 'You do not work in order to be satisfied, you do not work in order to have a life of ease; you have no business to be warm, you have no business to be at rest. Look at the peasants round about, they are hungry, it is for them that we must work, they are cold, it is for them that we must cut wood; they have many orphans, it is for them that you set up this orphanage; they are ignorant, it is for them that you have this school; the old people have no place to go, it is for them that you must maintain this old people's home.' And these poor thousand monks, some of whom were doing their utmost to be holy, groaned and groaned. . . And nevertheless, under the strong hand of their Superior they lived a life which was love. There were moments when they kicked, when the flesh weakened, but they had a conscience in their midst; it was St Joseph, who did not allow them to fall as low as they would have. To use more modern terminology, he is, if you like, a collective super-ego. He is there with his absolute demands. . . And here we have another monastic type.

Other monasteries of the same kind formed round him. Hunger, cold, ignorance, neglect of the aged, neglect of the young: all this became the object of love. And if you read the works and life of St Joseph, there is no doubt that there was nothing else but love, for he had no concern for anything else. He did not care about the consequences, nor did it matter what people thought of the folly of these things. What he said was that these people were hungry and in need of help, and that we who have known Christ, who know who He is, must bring Him to them. And if it costs you your life, well, it costs you your life! If you read his writings, you will see few reassuring passages on the repose which the monks will have and a much greater number in which they are warned that if they do not toil hard, there is hell fire.

After this epoch we find ourselves in a period in which States begin to acquire a reality which we would now call secular. The principality of Moscow begins to grow in strength and size. It devours the neighbouring principalities by most unworthy means and asserts a kind of ethic, a state law. At this moment the

Christian conscience rises up in a very curious way. At this period,
which was a time of renewal, when people were simply beginning
to breathe again and also to attach themselves more and more
to material goods—because they had begun to appear and
because everyone was happy to be able to build a livable world
at last—at this time a group of men and women, several dozen,
appeared successively and simultaneously, who were called 'God's
fools' or 'fools of Christ'. On close inspection the folly in question
can be interpreted in two different ways according to the
various cases. There was the folly undertaken by people of clear
intelligence, burning hearts and iron will. But there was also, in
certain cases, the holiness of those whose intelligence was
disturbed but who, basically, had God at the heart of their
interior life. They were people who denied all the social values:
wealth and the impossibility of living without many of the
material things so dear to man; the most primitive human
relations as well as the most demanding hierarchical relations.
They were men who, in this icy Russia of the North, walked the
streets with bare feet in winter, dressed only in a shirt, and
proclaimed the fact that if you believe, you can live by the Word
of God; *if you believe*, you can give up everything, whereas if
you let yourself become involved in the new tendency to accept
values that are only transitory, you are lost, you belong to the
world of Satan!

Was it an exaggeration or a vision of peace, a question of
depth? I believe there is a question of depth here. I have no wish
to say that we should all go out and do the same and that none
of the human values which the Christian world has formed in
the course of centuries have any meaning. But I believe that if
we have a religious vocation, if we have the sense of eternity, the
sense of the Presence—and if we know that God is living and
active in our midst and in us—we should have a Gospel on the
subject. It would consist in saying: 'Yes, all of that has a
temporary, transitory, ephemeral and sometimes even necessary
value taken as a whole, but we must not attach our hearts to it.
We must toil with our backs and our hands, but our heart
must not be put into it, for our heart should belong only
to God.'

Then a more complex situation enters into Russian history: the social life, the political life and the religious life mesh into one another in a way that is increasingly rich or increasingly impoverished, according to the moments. We find here all the types of Christian life that exist in the West, or in the Christian world taken as a whole, up to the moment when the Orthodox Church became the object of persecution in communist countries. At this moment the Church and the world become linked in a new way. If you think of the martyrs of the first centuries, you find that they are distinguished by certain characteristics. They were men, women and children who had discovered that God and Christ were the ultimate value for them, that in Him resided all the meaning of life. He was all in all to them. And it was out of personal loyalty that when His name was blasphemed, when His Person was put in question, they could only die for Him. On the other hand, in this relationship between Christ and those who believed in Him, a profound change was taking place in them: they would die to be reborn. Recall the 6th chapter of the Epistle to the Romans. They died the death of Christ and lived again by His Resurrection, they were in possession of eternal life, and it was eternal life that powerfully strengthened and gave direction to their temporal life. For them to die was not to perish but to be released from a transitory, ephemeral life with a view to attaining the fullness, the plenitude of eternal life in God. To live was Christ, but to die was a gain, for living in the flesh also meant being separated from God.

We see, however, that it was only indirectly, so to speak, that the martyrs brought about conversions: it was admiration, it was horror, it was the revelation of God by them which made conversions, but their intention seems to have been no more than to be witnesses of Christ, witnesses of the victory of God.

Since the revolution, in this world of incessant persecutions which are sometimes terrible and sharp, sometimes secret and hidden, a new mentality has developed. In this connection we can start with a thought that comes not from the Slavic world but from the West. Jean Daniélou says that suffering is the meeting-point of good and evil, of life and death. This is true, because evil is never something absolute, meta-physical and disincarnate: it always expresses itself in human persons, through human persons and to the detriment of human persons.

Evil always slashes, plunges into human flesh or into the human soul. There is always a person-to-person relationship where there is suffering, hate, greed or cowardice. But the victory is decisive: evil falls into the hands of the good, so to speak, because the moment we become victims, we acquire a right which is properly divine, to forgive. And then, just as Christ said, 'Father, forgive them, for they know not what they do,' so can we in our turn say, as one of our bishops did before his death in the course of the Stalinist purges: 'There will come a day when the martyr will be able to stand before the throne of God in defence of his persecutors and say, "Lord, I have forgiven in Thy Name and by Thy example: Thou hast no claim against them any more." '

This represents a new situation, a new mentality in the Church which is also one of the aspects of love, an aspect which surpasses our limits and is often too great for us because we are unable to do it on a small scale. How often are we able to forgive completely the little sufferings that are imposed upon us, the small sorrows inflicted on us? We have here a new upsurge of the love of God in human hearts, a new conquest by God. God manifests Himself once again, and the concept of the suffering Church and the personal martyr becomes at the same time a concept of the salvation of the other.

I hope that these examples will help you to grasp the fact that holiness is never in any way an individual act in the sense in which the word 'individual' signifies the lasts term of a fragmentation, the point beyond which one can no longer divide, and that holiness is always a situation and an act that imply not only the totality of the Church—since we are the living members of a body from which we cannot be separated and which cannot be separated from us—but also that we are members of the created world around us. Holiness is the love of God at work in a concrete, active, deliberate way, which applies itself with rigour and precision to situations that are always fresh and always contemporary with the eternal love of God and with the human presence of men, women and children who are possessed with this love and, being contemporaneous with their epoch, express it in a way that only they can choose, discover and put into practice.

The next point I wish to take up is one which, I think, is very important for the way in which we evaluate the world and our situation in the world: it is the notion of the *solidarity of God with the world*. I purposely use the word 'solidarity', which is neither theological nor pious, in order to avoid using a word, whatever it might be, that would put us right into an old rut where we could resolve without effort an extremely sharp and important problem.

When we come to the subject of prayer in its relationship to holiness I shall try to give enough emphasis to the aspect of holiness which is oriented wholly towards God and whose sole content is God. Before doing that, I think it would be best to take a brief look at man, who is the object of incarnate holiness, the one towards whom the instances of human holiness are directed and with whom they often deal.

Two notions have come to the fore, since the war, perhaps, more than in the years that preceded it; the notion of the greatness of man, of his significance both for us men and for God, and the notion of human solidarity. For centuries, it seems, within the Church we have tried to make our God as great as we could, by making man small. This can be seen even in works of art in which the Lord Jesus Christ is represented as great and his creatures as very small indeed at his feet. The intention was to show how great God was, and yet it has resulted in the false and almost blasphemous view that man is small or, on the other hand, in the denial of this God who treats men as though they were of no value. And these two reactions are equally wrong. The one belongs to people who claim to be children of God, God's own chosen people, who are the Church. They have managed by doing this to make themselves as small as the image they have of men, and their communities as small and lacking in scope and greatness as their constitutive parts. The other attitude we find outside the Church, among the agnostics, the rationalists and the atheists. But in these reactions we find a common ground—man—who is now a point of real and extremely fruitful encounter between those who hold the two most clearly opposed ideologies: faith and atheism. Man is the only object which they have in common. They visualise him and treat him differently, but the fact remains that it is man who is at the centre of both schools of thought. One could almost say that the modern interpretation of St Paul's encounter with that altar 'to the unknown God' would be to say that the unknown god is man, whom everyone is placing on the altar now. The atheist world sets up the empirical man and the collective man. The Christian world also places a man on the altar: the man Jesus Christ. The fact that the breadth of the vision of man in Christianity exceeds all the bounds of the created does not keep Jesus, the Son of God, the Word Incarnate, from being fully man in the total sense of the word 'fully'.

I repeat a point already made. Marx says that the proletariat has no need of a god because man has become his god. And St John Chrysostom: 'If you want to measure the greatness of man, raise your eyes towards the throne of God and you will see the Word Incarnate, the bearer of our humanity, seated at the right hand of the glory.' Here are the two clearest expressions of the modern situation. And yet in both cases it is man who is at the centre of everything.

For the atheist world—I mean the atheist world that has an ideology, not the atheist world of the stomach which one might call 'gastric' atheism, about whom St Paul is speaking when he tells us, 'These men's god is their belly'—for the ideological atheist who bases himself on a conception of the world, theoretical man is truly a god. One might even ask what is the extent of this reality of the man-god for the atheist. The striking thing is that, on the one hand, the theoretical man is a god; at the same time the empirical man is a victim and a slave. This, I think, is explained by the fact that the theoretical man in question who is placed on the altar of atheism is not a personal man, he is not each man considered in his person, which is not only inimitable but also unique, but it is the collective man. And this theoretical-collective man, who is unique, challenges the rights of the individual man. The former is the man of the present and the future, not the concrete man living in the present nor the individual man who will live in the future, but humanity—or the 'class'—and this is always a collectivity which has the right to make absolute demands on each of its members. In the matter of art, literature, civic conduct and conscientious inner conviction, this collectivity has totalitarian claims. And the concrete man, the individual, whose human course proceeds as if made up of little pieces like a mosaic, has only his small place in it: he cannot go beyond the place assigned to him; he only has the right to possess the position and colour that are imposed upon him.

It is necessary to emphasise very strongly the profound difference between the atheist notion of the collective and the notion of the Church, in which we are members of a living body; likewise between the notion of the 'individual' and that of the 'person' which is the condition of man within the Church.

The collective position is that in which an ideological minority becomes a *de facto* majority, having the right to impose its will on each member of the society. In the Church there is nothing of the sort. Even the will and word of God have no authority in the sense of a law which is imposed. It is a voice which reveals to us the reality and truth of things. If we respond to it, we do so because we are sensitive to the truth of what is proclaimed to us and we reach out towards this reality, which is the only means we have of becoming fully free and fully ourselves. The will of God is not a law nor an imprisonment. One of our Russian theologians of the 19th century, Khomyakov, who was one of the most passionate polemicists against Catholicism and Protestantism at the same time—and from this point of view was not exactly a forerunner of ecumenism—tells us that the will of God is a malediction for the demon, it is the law for unregenerate man, and freedom for those who have attained salvation.

In these terms, which are perfectly adequate to the theme, we see that it is not a question of a will imposed from outside, but of a will that appears external to us in the measure in which we ourselves are external to our vocation and to our human reality. On the other hand, in the atheist world of the collectivity it is a will of iron that is imposed on its members: it pours scorn on the convictions and the most categorical imperatives of conscience, because the truth is expressed by the Party, or else by such and such a human group that considers itself to be in possession of the truth and of the right to define it according to needs and convention. In this view man is seen as an individual who has no supra-personal life, no life that transcends him and means that he lives in others and others in him; he forms part of a gear, he is one of the constituent but replaceable elements.

We see the tragic working of this not only in the Russian Revolution in its full scope but even in the story of the members of the Party in the time of the Stalinist purges. One can read the book by Eugenie Ginsburg, who was a member of the Party before the revolution, passionately devoted to her party, and who spent eighteen years in concentration camps simply because she refused to sign a list of statements of confession to crimes that she had never committed but which were useful at the moment to her party's line.

According to Marxist ideology, the individual is an interchangeable being; in contrast, the person is unique and irreplaceable: this is a profound difference that exists within and outside the Church. It is important in the matter of holiness, because each of us is unique, irreplaceable, and only knows God in a unique way that no one else could share. The replaceable individual, towards whom the work of holiness on the part of the Church is directed, should be transformed into that which he really is: a human person. I should like to indicate briefly the difference between these two terms by saying again that an individual is the last term of a fragmentation: it is not possible to divide further than the individual. If you endeavour to go further in your attempt at dissection, you will get a corpse and a soul: you will no longer be in the presence of the whole human being.

The person is altogether different: this can best be defined by the passage from the Book of Revelation in which we are told that in the Kingdom of God each of those who enter will receive a white stone with a name inscribed on it—a name known only to God and to the one who receives it. This name is not the nickname by which we are known in ordinary life—surname, Christian name—it is a name that contains, and defines all that we are and all that we are called to be. We can imagine it to be the mysterious word that God uttered in order to call us into being out of nothingness, out of the radical absence from which we were drawn by the will of God. This name, which defines us completely and is known only to God and the one who bears it, defines the unique, unprecedented and unparalleled relationship that each of us has with God. In his relationship persons are not opposable, individuals are indeed: we recognise them by opposing traits of character, external features, psychological and social traits; we speak of their colour, stature, weight, nationality. Here the question does not concern those things: it is a question of something very profound and unique, such that it is not by contrast nor by opposition nor comparison that we recognise the human person, but by the fact that he is himself and that no one has ever been nor ever will be what he is, because if two persons could be identified with one another, they would be one. Thus we see clearly that the collective, which deals with individuals, and the Church, which is composed of members who are living, unique, irreplaceable and incomparable with one another, are profoundly different realities. Holiness belongs to the sphere of the Church as a body and to the sphere of the person, while it is completely alien to the categories of the individual, who by definition is contrasted and distinguished, and of the collectivity, which asserts itself and limits the individual's own possibilities.

So if we as the Church are called to be a human presence of the kind that can be described in terms of sociology or history, we must nevertheless remember that this human presence is not the presence of an ordinary society. It is not only the place of the presence of God, it is also that of the presence of man, seen, conceived, lived in a unique way which is unknown to the world. And in our missionary work, in our enlargement of the limits of the holiness of the Church and of man in particular, if we lose sight of this, if we forget that it is God, and man in God, who is the object of holiness, we have lost sight of the essential. We can create organisations which are more or less useful—and they will certainly be replaced some day by more effective social organisations, because the possibilities of the total *socius* are greater than those of the particular society that we are—but we will never attain the goal which is offered to us, to be this revelation of the holiness of God, Who is winning and assimilating the world to Himself, making us participants in the divine nature and temples of the Holy Spirit, the really living Body of Christ, and making our life hidden in God with Jesus Christ.

Thus the element of holiness in the Church is found to be connected with a two-fold vision of man, but one that is different from that of the world. In this confrontation, this encounter between ourselves and the world outside, we must make our contribution to what man is—and we cannot accept the vision of a secular holiness which knows nothing of the depths of man, of his bond with God, and which defines holiness in moral and pragmatic or practical categories.

In the Church we have a two-fold vision of man: empirical man and the man revealed in Jesus Christ. There is also the corollary fact that the Church is simultaneously a society in history and, invisibly yet transparently, a mystery. From the empirical point of view we are the Church, all of us such as we are, not only such as we are called to be, but as we are in the frailty of the individual and in the insufficiency and implenitude of human becoming. From this point of view the Church can be defined in the terms used by St Ephraim the Syrian in the sixth century: 'The Church is not the assembly of saints, it is the mass of sinners who repent, who, sinners though they are, have turned towards God and are oriented towards Him.' From this point of view it is true that the Church is the object of history and of sociological studies, because from that aspect it belongs to the world, for it has not yet been liberated by holiness from the world's grasp. The world is within it through us in so far as each of us is not freed from the world, in the ascetic sense.

But on the other hand, there is in the Church a vision of man which is not a theory of man. It is not the ideal man, it is not the invented man, nor man as we wish he were, and towards which we aim as a sort of created transcendence. No, it is a real man really revealed, for it must never be forgotten that among the people who form the Church of the Living God there is one such man, Jesus, the incarnate God, true man in the double sense of the word: he is true in the sense that he is in nothing different from us, he is not a superman, not a man who appeared in our midst from outside. He is flesh of our flesh, bone of our bone; he belongs to us entirely, just as we belong to him entirely. That is why we can say, even with regard to the human existence of the Church, that we believe in the Church, for in Christ it is an object of faith, a vision of man which is not the empirical reality and which nevertheless already is empirical reality, because it is an empirical reality that we can observe in history. True man, in the fullness of reality, has appeared to us in the Person of Christ, the Word Incarnate, a man who is genuine in the fullest sense of the word. Among Orthodox and Catholics I will also add that we have a vision of true man in the Holy Virgin, who attained the fullness of her human vocation, as witnessed by our common faith in the Assumption, that is to say, in her bodily resurrection.

Since that time, for the people of the Church, to be a man has meant seeking this identification with the Christ-Man in the same way as he accepted his identification with the empirical man that we had become by our fall and that we are by definition in the created world. Thus action, service and contemplation within the Church are correlative and linked necessarily with one another, for it is only to the extent to which we can see, that we can grow to the measure of that which we see. Only to the extent that we can see and hear the God-man in action can we act in conformity with the divine plan and take our part in the world.

As our holiness can only find its place in the created world where we are—I do not speak of society, because the anchorites and hermits are equally a part of the Church and have their part to play in the created world—it is only as far as we can see and hear, that we can act, or rather *be*, according to the will of God, so that our being is a creative and saving act, an act of holiness that would be our sanctification but is also a sanctification for the entire world. Here is where the notion of wisdom has its special place. It is a wisdom different from human sagacity. We see it in the prophets and patriarchs and New Testament saints: their inner capacity for profound peace, for absolute stability, for gazing earnestly and patiently at the world in which they lived in order to discern in it the trace of the passage of

God, the way He followed, in order to follow that way, for it is He alone Who is the Way. And it is on this way that we can find and give the Truth and the Life.

This necessity of looking and seeing is expressed in a way which I find very beautiful in a narrative told by Nathaniel Hawthorne, relating a New World legend. In a village built on a high mountain cut by a stream and facing the little cluster of huts, very high up in the rock, a face has been carved in the rock from time immemorial; it is the face of the god of these villagers. It is a face of transcendent beauty, expressing an ineffable peace and complete harmony. And the villagers hand down a promise from generation to generation that there will come a day when this god will detach himself from the mountain and live among them. They admire this face, they are inspired by it—and they fall back again and again into the cares of their poor community life. However, one day a child is born in the village who, from the moment he was capable of seeing, perceiving and responding, of submitting to external impressions, as soon as he could crawl from the hut where he was born down to the edge of the stream, was struck by the beauty, serenity and majesty of this face. One could always find him sitting beside the stream doing nothing but looking.

The years pass, the baby becomes a little boy and later a young man. A day comes when the inhabitants of the village, seeing him pass by, stop and exclaim, 'Our god is in our midst!' By thrusting his gaze deep into this face he had become inwardly conformed to the whole expression and spiritual content of this other face, by gazing at it he had become imbued with it, he had allowed himself to be penetrated by the serenity, the grandeur, peace and love which radiated from that face of stone. And now his face had become that of the god whom he had venerated and quite simply gazed at.

I believe that there is something essential here in terms of holiness and also in terms of the place which human holiness can have within a complex pluralist society like that in which we live. If only we knew how to gaze with all the depths of our being at the face of Christ, that invisible face which we can see only by turning towards our own depths and which we see emerging from there, then those around us would relive the impact of a serenity, a deepening, a peace, a power both strong and gentle, and they would understand that there is holiness in the Church. And this holiness would have no need to make desperate efforts to manifest itself in order to make others believe that the Church is holy. Everyone would believe—which is so difficult to do when one looks at us!

All holiness is God's holiness in us: it is a holiness that is participation and, in a certain way, more than participation, because as we participate in what we can receive from God, we become a revelation of that which transcends us. Being a limited light, we reveal the Light. But we should also remember that in this life in which we are striving towards holiness, our spirituality should be defined in very objective and precise terms. When we read books on spirituality or engage in studying the subject, we see that spirituality, explicitly or implicitly, is repeatedly defined as an attitude, a state of soul, an inner condition, a type of interiority, and so on. In reality, if you look for the ultimate definition and try to discover the inner core of spirituality, you find that spirituality does not consist of the states of soul that are familiar to us, but that it is the presence and action of the holy spirit in us, by us and through us in the world. It is not fundamentally a matter of the way in which we express it.

There is an absolute objectivity both to holiness and to the spirituality which is expressed in it. Spirituality is that of the Spirit; didn't St Paul tell us that it is the holy Spirit who teaches us to say: 'Abba, Father'? Doesn't he mean that it is the holy Spirit, God Himself, who shapes in us the knowledge of God? And, furthermore, there is no other holiness than that of God; it is as the Body of Christ that we can participate in holiness, in Christ and in the holy Spirit.

If such is the case, a question of tremendous importance arises. In view of our search for holiness, in as much as it is situated, whether we like it or not, within the framework of the created world and the world of men, the tragic, complex world in which we live— if it is the presence of Christ Himself and the inspiration of the Spirit which the holiness of the Church should express in each of its members and in the totality of its body, *where is the limit of this love*? In other words, where is the limit of our sense of solidarity and responsibility? Is there a moment when we should detach ourselves and say: 'I leave you, go your way; if you repent, if you change, we will find one another again, but as you are, I can no longer go with you.' Or are there no limits, not only to God's condescension but also to this tremendous and passionate solidarity of God? Holy Scripture more than once places us in the presence of God's love in terms of 'Eros', that is, a love and attachment that is total and passionate, which embraces everything, leaving nothing outside.

I should like to draw your attention to a quotation which is certainly not scriptural and has no authority in itself, but which seems interesting to me. In the seventeenth century a Russian priest, a man of burning convictions, wrote his autobiography. He wanted to show how a man of faith can remain faithful to what he believes to be the truth in spite of the treachery, or what he considered to be the treachery of the visible Church. A prologue is attached to this *Vita*, written by himself. At one point in it he speaks of the divine Council which preceded the creation of the world and says: 'In the light of what we know of God Incarnate, can we not say that one day the Father said to the Son: "My Son, let us create a visible world and man." And the Son replies: "My Father, let it be according to Thy Will." And the Father adds: "My Son, you know that if I make it through you, there will come a time when man will play us false and in order to bring him back to us you will have to die?" And the Son replies: "Let it be according to Thy Will, my Father!" And the world was created.' This is not apocryphal, in as much as it makes no pretence of expressing a scriptural reality in other terms, but it expresses a profound inner reality: God in His divine Wisdom willed and called the world into being in full awareness of the consequences which this divine call, which made a free world appear out of nothing, would have for God Himself. This is a contest between God and the world, if we may say so, and the tragedy we so often complain about is more tragic for God than for the world!

Throughout the history of the Old and New Testaments we

see how God afterwards takes His full responsibility for His creative act. Step by step he upholds the prophets, declares His will, reveals the depth of His thought. Didn't Amos say that the prophet is he with whom God shares His thoughts? And He remains faithful when creation has become unfaithful—remember Hosea and the images he gives of the faithful husband of a woman who has deserted him. So underlying everything there is a unilateral act of God, but it is an act for which He takes total and final responsibility. This is important because if we are 'in God', we must share with Him, at least take our part of this divine responsibility. Our election to be the Church is not a paradisiac privilege. It is basically an election to share the thought and heart of God, but also to share Christ's work in the Incarnation and the economy of salvation. I want here to insist on the intensity of this solidarity, simply turning your thought to those words of Christ, almost the last ones he uttered on the Cross: 'My God, my God, why hast Thou forsaken me?'

When we speak of the solidarity of Christ with men in the Incarnation, we continually think of the minor and major expressions of this contradiction. We consider the limitations which the divine Word imposed upon Himself in entering time and becoming a prisoner of space: He is hungry, thirsty, tired: On another level, He seeks, He accepts the company of sinners. He lives in the midst of hatred and this hatred kills Him at a certain moment. These last two terms seem very weak to me, and this is their weakness: 'human hatred kills him'. This prevents people from understanding what is special about the death of Christ. If it is in terms of death, all those who have attained mortality die, and He did nothing that each of us will not have to do some day. If it is in terms of suffering, there are millions of people who have suffered infinitely more than He on the cross. Two thieves were crucified at the same time as He, they also died a human death on the cross. If we think of the 11th chapter of the Epistle to the Hebrews, we see that human suffering, human horror, even in terms of holiness, has surpassed all that we can imagine of the physical suffering of Christ. The tragedy of His death is not His ultimate participation in human tragedy and human destiny.

The unique human tragedy, the only one that counts, the one out of which all the others arise, is mortality, and this mortality is linked with sin, with separation from God. And it is here that the death of Christ and his solidarity with us contain something more frightful than we can imagine. St Maximus the Confessor says in his Study of the Incarnation: 'It is unthinkable that human flesh that is united indissolubly for ever with Divinity could, even as human flesh, be mortal.' To be mortal means to be separated. And he stresses the fact that from the moment of the Incarnation Jesus of Nazareth, by reason of the union of divinity with humanity, was immortal, free of the necessity of death. His death is not only a simple acceptance of the human condition; it is conditioned by the ultimate experience of the human tragedy, which consists in losing God and dying because of this. Here we have something extremely important: Christ in his Incarnation accepted not only the limitations but the depth of our tragedy. According to the old saying what Christ has not participated in remains outside the mystery of salvation. If Christ had not participated in our break with God, in our estrangement, in what one of our theologians called a psychological eclipse which made him lose sight of the presence of God, he would not have participated fully in our mortality, and our mortality would have been outside the mystery of the Redemption.

Thus we see how far divine love goes in this solidarity with us: Christ accepts not only being like one of us, not only participating in everything except sin, but in participating even in 'estrangement', in the fact of becoming a stranger, of withdrawing from the Father in order to participate in the unique tragedy of man: atheism.

The same idea is expressed in the Apostles' Creed, when we say, 'He descended into Hell.' Since Dante we have thought of a hell of torments: but the Hell spoken of in the Old Testament is not a hell of torments: it is Sheol, which is simply the place where every human soul is cut off, the place where God is not, because before Christ's Redemption there is a gulf between God and man which only the Redemption, the Christ-mystery can fill. He descends into Hell. Hell opens wide to seize a new prey in whom to press a final victory over God, without knowing whom it is receiving. And into this Hell which receives a man God Himself enters. I believe there is a final touch here which explains what the psalmist has a foreboding of when he exclaims: 'Whither should I flee before Thy face? To Heaven? But that is Thy abode! To Hell? But Thou art there also!' Nothing in the condition of the created, nothing in the condition of man, except sin, is now outside the experience of Christ, outside the reality of Christ. Everything is contained in him, and there is not an atheist in the world who has known atheism, the loss of God, in the way Christ, the Son of Man has, who died on the cross with that cry of ultimate anguish and agony. Here again we see the breadth of divine love and the depth of this acceptance by God of everything which is the human condition. 'Nothing human is alien to me,' said Tertullian. Perhaps he did not know how far this acceptance of the human condition went for God. He died. He died without sin. With what death did he die? With ours, with a borrowed death. Is not this the divine vocation, to remain without sin and to die a borrowed death?

I should like now to speak about prayer in connection with what has been said so far about holiness. Prayer and holiness seem to me to be rooted in a twofold experience, not in two experiences but in a twofold, correlative one. On the one hand there is the amazement that we feel in the short—but real—moments when we perceive God, when we almost touch the hem of His garment; these moments of wonder are flashing instants of contemplation, and they leave us in a contemplative state, in deepening prayer, meditation and interiority which are on the border of profound contemplation and life in God. On the other hand, at the other pole of this twofold reality of prayer and holiness we find despair and compassion: despair such as we see, for instance, at the end of the 10th chapter of St Mark, the despair of blind Bartimaeus at the gate of Jericho, the despair of a man who has been blind and has suffered from it, who has fought for his sight for years and finally, crushed by misfortune, has settled into his blindness. And then suddenly he hears that there is a man living in Galilee in Judaea who has the power to give sight to a man born blind, to cure every sickness, to heal every infirmity. And this man is passing his way. And this moment when the last hope is passing by is a moment of reawakening of all the feelings of despair that he bears within him as well as all the hope of which he is capable.

We can pray at moments when we become aware of our blindness—and we can include in this term whatever makes us blind to God and to all that surrounds us—and when we sense that the One who can cure us is passing near. Prayer arises at moment when we become deeply aware of our separation and of the fact that our life is suspended over death, that nothingness is within us and lapping round us from all sides, ready to engulf us. And when we turn our gaze towards others, in place of that despair linked to an ultimate hope, which is the hope that Bartimaeus had, it is compassion which awakes in us, the capacity to suffer deeply, intensely, not the suffering of the other—for one can never suffer the suffering of another nor ever understand another —but one can suffer from the fact that he is suffering, and in a mysterious way, beyond all experience, participate within this unity of the Body of Christ, in the common suffering which is his.

There is a link between *contemplation and intercession*, between the contemplation of God and this active, concrete prayer directed to the present and to .the world in which we live. A Russian monk from a monastery which is now in Finland had spent fifty years in his monastery without consenting to make profession, saying: 'I am unworthy, I don't yet know how to love. . .' And when he was asked: 'But what would you say a monk is, after all?' he answered: 'A monk is one who can weep for the whole world'. Here you see a man who had spent fifty years in a completely contemplative life, not oriented towards anything—in the last twenty years of his life he was bedridden because in the course of his work he had lost an arm, had lost a leg, had become blind—and nevertheless he refused the monastic profession because it seemed impossible for him to love and be a monk, that is, to be alone with God, not in a withdrawn solitude but in ardent and active solitude. Thus there is a bond which does not allow a separation between *contemplation in prayer*, the adoration of God, and *action*, the prayer of intercession or physical presence. But it is only to the extent to which our physical presence is the presence of God through us, the presence of Eternity in time through us, that we remain the Church while remaining engaged in action. If our activity in the world becomes a disengagement in relation to God, we fall back into the condition of a human society which has an ideology but no transcendent reality.

If we want to be active and contemplative at the same time, if we want to follow the line of holiness or communion with divine life, in a profound, intense, creative way while being at the same time in the midst of the world, whether in a cloistered order—for the cloister is now more than ever incapable of being radically set apart—or actively engaged in life, we must learn a way of prayer that permits inner stability—not psychological stability (which we lack, but the problem is not in that, nor is the solution to be found on that level), but an inner stability which consists of standing immobile, face to face with the living God. We must attain to a prayer of presence, our presence with God and his presence in the world through us. This is one of the aspects of intercession.

I should like to say a few words about this aspect in order to be able to use it in what follows. I should like to give you the story of the Wedding at Cana as an example of intercessory prayer defined as a presence.

You know the scene: a village wedding, poor and simple, with Christ, the Mother of God and his disciples who have been invited. Long before hearts have been seized with joy, long before they are overflowing with that life, the human conditions for joy begin to run out. No doubt the lights are going dim, the bread has been eaten and the wine is failing. At this moment the Holy Virgin makes an act of presence, not in the vulgar sense in which we speak of putting on an act as distinct from inner involvement,—but she makes the act of being there, fully and completely involved. As you will see, she is involved exactly in that twofold way which makes *contemplation active and action contemplative*. She turns to the Lord and says to Him: 'They have no more wine.' What is Mary asking? Would she really like the Lord to perform an act of magic and multiply the wine until the guests had drunk so much that they fell asleep under the tables? Is this

the joy that she wants for them? It is unthinkable. So there is
something more in it; there is a premonition, a foreknowledge
of the fact that if Christ gives them what the earth is now
refusing, the gift will be one that is at the same time of the order
of eternal life. Christ then turns to her and asks her a question:
'What have you and I in common? My hour has not come.' I
know that there are pious translations which try to avoid a
sentence that seems incomprehensible and difficult, that seems
to be an insult to the holy Virgin, and they do their best to trans-
late this sentence too briefly to be perfectly clear semantically,
by saying: 'What does it matter to you and me?' But 'What does
it matter to us' would be an atrocious thing for Christ to say.
'What is it to me that their joy is fading, what is it to me that this
party isn't finished and doesn't reach its perfection? Haven't we
who are sober had enough to eat?' Is that what he means?
Certainly not, for 'My hour has not yet come' is a statement that
pertains to eternal life and the coming of the Kingdom, and not
simply to the magistery of a miracle-worker. 'What is there in
common between you and me?' How are we to understand this
sentence? St John Chrysostom comments on it in a way that
seems to me more than strange: I believe he is in line with a
certain modern psychology which always sees all the faults on the
side of the parents. Here, according to him, not even the holy
Virgin has escaped this tendency of all mothers to believe that
because they have brought a child into the world, they have
imprescriptible rights over him until his death. So there she is
intruding, giving herself rights. . . and Christ puts her back in her
place. Saint though he is, I believe that in this case St John
Chrysostom, not through any lack of devotion, has misunder-
stood the text. Other commentaries seem to me more adequate.
'What have you and I in common? Why is it you who make
this request? Is it because you are my mother according to the
flesh that you feel you have rights over me?' (We are in line
with St John Chrysostom.) Or 'Has everything that you learned
from the angel, everything that you kept in your heart and
pondered in the course of your life, revealed to you that "I am
here", a presence which makes this human marriage unfold to
the dimensions of the Wedding of the Lamb? If you are speaking

to me because you are my mother according to the flesh, my hour has not yet come.' He leaves the question hanging. The holy Virgin does not answer: 'Am I not your mother? Don't you know how much faith I have in you?' She only answers him with a gesture, but it is much more convincing than all the phrases she could have uttered. She turns to the servants and says to them: 'Whatever he tells you to do, do it.' She makes a total, integral, unlimited act of faith, the faith on which the Annunciation was founded; the faith that she bore witness to in being the mother of the Child-God now comes to light in all its fullness. Because she believed in a perfect way, she established at this instant, in this village wedding, the Kingdom of God. For the Kingdom of God is that in which we offer to God with a pure heart a faith without blemish. There is an old saying of Israel: 'God is everywhere man permits Him to enter.' The holy Virgin, by this act of faith, established the conditions of the Kingdom and opened to God the doors of this village wedding. So it turns out that the hour of the Lord has come: it is the hour of the Kingdom, where everything is in harmony with God because man has believed. He blesses the exhausted waters, the useless waters, the waters soiled by washing, and transforms them into the wine of the Kingdom, into a revelation of something greater, which makes this wedding that had begun as a human event unfold to the measure of the Kingdom of God.

You see what this presence and this holiness can be: the presence of God, because one human person was present to God. When this takes its place in the world of the Church, we find ourselves in the presence of the People of God, which is the very place of the Presence. If we wish to pray within this situation, we must learn to pray in *stability and silence:* stability in the sense that we must find a way of praying while standing face to face in the immobility and deepening of silence, contemplation, wonder and anguish that are due to God's Presence. The reason we so often lose this Presence is that our very prayer, not only our life, keeps moving and shifting. We start with one idea and turn towards another; we continually change our terms of reference. God remains Himself constantly, but we offer Him prayer that is always changing, always expressing the external and internal changes, and even conditions them. If we say discursive prayers, we have to adjust our heart and spirit along a line that is often very complex and greatly lacking in sobriety in certain cases, whether the prayers are our own—often much too rich and ornate —or we find them in the Christianity of the Middle Ages or that of Byzantine rhetoric.

So it is first of all a question of establishing ourselves before God. And this is by no means different from action or incompatible with it, because the sense of internal tension, the sense of haste and of movement are internal states that are not connected with the circumstances of our life. You have surely seen people who are old or infirm loaded with a suitcase and trying with all possible speed to catch a bus that is about to leave. They hurry desperately. And nevertheless, objectively, their movement is slow and heavy, their change of position minimal. You also know how easy it is for us sometimes when we are on holiday, when we are not striving towards any concrete goal, to feel wholly within ourselves, collected. One of the fifth century Fathers said that we must establish ourselves firmly inside our skin with nothing protruding outside. At the same time we are full of vivacity, we move fast and are capable of acting quickly. Why? Because we are not reaching after anything, the aim and content of our life in this situation is to be where we are now, whereas ordinarily, and nearly all the time, we live as if we were trying to catch a bus.

We have an erroneous notion of time. The amazing thing in life, said a seventeenth century Russian philosopher, is that all the necessary things are simple and all the complicated things are useless. In fact, if we could only remember that time does not run away, that at a slow pace or at a gallop it rushes towards us, we should be much less fearful of losing it. Do you think that by going towards the hour of your death as fast as possible you can prevent it from coming, or catch it? Do you think that if you go on placidly, tranquilly listening to me, the hour of your deliverance will not come? In both cases it is time which is coming towards you, you have no need to run after it.

It is coming. . . and you will not escape it any more than it will escape you. Therefore we can establish ourselves quite peacefully where we are, knowing that if the time ahead has a meaning that is necessary for us, it is inevitably coming towards us at a sure and regular pace, sometimes much more quickly than we could run to meet it.

On the other hand, if we establish ourselves peacefully in the present, we are living in a world of realities, whereas if we hurry towards the future, we are moving towards a world of unreality. I think the importance of this is truly essential. We must know how to use time, the time within which we find—at least we can find—all eternity, for eternity and time are incommensurable with one another. Eternity is not an indefinite length of time; eternity is not the presence of time without end. The difference between time and eternity is that time is a category of the created: it appears at the moment when something which did not exist before begins to be and to become, and it exists as long as the becoming continues. Eternity does not answer the question: 'What?' It answers the question 'Who?' Eternity is God, God who is always contemporaneous with each moment of time; He is always there, completely stable, unchanged and unchangeable because He already has in Himself, before the first thing was, all the richness necessary to meet all things and all situations. He does not need to change in order to be contemporaneous.

If we wish to learn this prayer of stability, then, we must first realise that it is useless to look for God within a time. He is in the time in which we are, He is in every instant, every 'twinkling of an eye', to use a formula of Romano Guardini's, who distinguishes the past, the future and, not the present, which seems to him too thick, but the 'twinkling of an eye', the instant which has hardly appeared before it is gone. If we want to draw upon this prayer of stability, we must learn to manage time. We always know how to manage time when it is not a matter of God or of prayer; we do not know how when it concerns eternity! This remarkable, illogical situation is the constant experience of each one of us. Take, for example, what you do when you get on a train: you install yourself as comfortably as possible, you are at ease. From within this repose you look around you, you read, you speak, you think, I suppose you sometimes even pray . . . and you worry about nothing because you know that the train will arrive at the destination no matter what you do.

There are some rather simple and nervous people who sometimes try to go from the last carriage to the first in order to be a little closer to their destination. Those who have a little more sense realise that two hundred meters out of fifteen hundred kilometers make no essential difference and that one can simply allow oneself a few hours' rest. Why do we never do this in prayer? Isn't it remarkable that we should find this the most natural thing in the world when it is a matter of getting to another place, simply because we are sure of what is happening as far as the train is concerned—and yet there are so many possible hazards—and we are never sure of what is going to happen with God! It feels to us as though unless we are quick, mistrustful and active, He will escape us. In fact, in a certain way He does escape us. And that is not because we do not look for Him but because we look for Him everywhere where He is not. From this point of view Bonhoeffer is with us when he says that Christianity is a religion without religion, if we understand by the word 'religion' a system of methods that make it possible to catch God, to take Him captive, to get Him in a trap and keep Him there. Yes, in this case Christianity, and only Christianity, is a religion without religion, gecause God wanted to make Himself interior to our condition, and He wanted us to have no need to try to hold Him captive, Who became flesh in order to be with us. There is no need for us to try to use methods and techniques to make Him our prisoner.

Not only is He in our midst, but He created this Church, which is not just a human society oriented towards God, for it is the place of His Presence, the mystery of the union with God, an organism which is simultaneously and equally human and divine, where the plenitude of God resides with the implenitude of men, leading little by little towards that accomplishment in which God will be all in all and the Church will encompass all things.

Hence it is a necessity for us to learn to master time in this way. For this there are techniques, techniques addressed to our restlessness, to our incapacity to believe in the Word of God Who has promised to be with us until the end of the ages.

The first thing we could do is to compel ourselves to place ourselves in the Presence of God and to remain there a few moments without trying to escape—and without trying to give to this presence a discursive content, whether of emotions or of thoughts. If you sit down in a room and say to yourself: 'I am in the presence of God', you will see that at the end of a moment you will be wondering how to fill this presence with an activity that will suppress your restlessness. For the first few moments you will feel fine because you are tired and it is a rest to be sitting comfortably in an armchair, and the silence of your room gives you a feeling of quietude. All this is true. But if you have to go beyond this moment of natural rest, and you remain in the presence of God when you have already received from physical nature all that you can get from it, you will see that it is very difficult not to wonder: 'And now what shall I do? What should I say to God? How shall I address Him? He is silent. Is He there? How can I make a bridge between that mute absence and my restless presence?'

So one of the first things to understand is the importance of sitting and doing nothing in front of God. This does not seem very pious, and yet if you arrive at that repose which the mystical Greek Fathers at Mt Athos called 'Hesychia', a word that has given rise to a whole tradition, hesychasm, the tradition of the Jesus Prayer, a tradition of silent and contemplative prayer—if you reach that, then within that silence and immobility you will be able to do something.

But this immobility and silence, this presence with God must be learned. If you have learned it, you can try to do more difficult exercises: 1) make your presence with God a little longer; 2) learn to manage time, not when it is moving in a sluggish, meandering way, but at the moment when it is trying to rush like water from a burst pipe. It is simply a matter of saying at the moment when you are busy with something useful which must be done: 'I stop doing this, I'll keep still an instant and remain alone with God! All that I am doing can wait!' The Russians, who are not oppressively active people when they can avoid it, have a point of view which I think has spiritual value. One said to me: 'It is so wonderful: I can always be unhurried because if I do not die immediately I shall have time to do it, and if I die, it is useless for me to do it!'

Ask this question: Does the salvation of the world truly depend on the letter that you are writing, the copper you are cleaning, the sentence full of wisdom that you are in the midst of pronouncing? Did the world not exist for millions of years before you said or did this or that? Will it not still live millions of years without your continuing to be a useful presence? So give it a chance now to enjoy your absence. Settle peacefully and say: 'Whatever happens, I will not budge.' Say to all those, visible and invisible, who come to disturb you: 'I am very sorry; I am here, but not for you! . . .' This is what we are always doing: suppose we are in conversation with someone and another person knocks on the door, you answer: 'I am sorry, I am busy.' If you are busy with God, you do not say: 'I am sorry, go away.' What logic, what common sense is there in this? It is not even a matter of contemplation, it is a matter of being polite!

Learn to remain in interior repose, peacefully and tranquilly, in spite of the telephone, in spite of someone's knocking at the door, in spite of the demon's saying to you: 'And you have forgotten this. . .; you still have to get this done by such-and-such an hour. . .; and the brass is not shiny enough, the sun is brighter than it. . . and if you added this sentence to your letter, you would be doing something worthy of the Fathers and Mothers of the Church.' But you answer him: 'If this comes from God, He will be quite able to remind me at an appropriate time, if it comes from you, I mistrust it. . .'

If you learn to stop time, to manage it in this way one, two, three, ten times a day, for longer and longer moments, you will come to the time when you can do it at any time, no matter what your activity, no matter what the word or thought, whether in the liturgy or in everyday life. . . Thus you will be able to be interior to yourself, constantly face to face with God, asking Him unceasingly what you must do, what you must listen to. You will be fundamentally in the position of a monk or a nun: obedience, which consists of *ob-audire*, listening, listening with the intention of hearing—which is not always what we intend when we listen to our neighbour—of understanding what he says, of grasping what he wanted to say and of perceiving the depths from which this word came and what it is meant to make us discover.

I remember something my grandmother told me when I was a child. She was talking to me about the Greek war of independence against Turkey. . . and she told the case of a soldier who, after the battle, in the dark night, called his lieutenant and cried: 'Lieutenant, lieutenant, I have taken a prisoner!'—'Bring him here,' answered the lieutenant.—'I can't, he is holding me so tight,' replied the soldier. This seems absurd. . . and yet I have the impression that very often it is the situation in which we find ourselves with respect to the world when we who are prisoners of this world in a thousand ways—not so much outwardly as inwardly—think that we can transform it, and we are aware that we can only begin to do it when we try to change our place and pull the world in our direction instead of staying in the midst of it where it is and imagining that our presence is enough to be a miracle of transfiguration. There is something very important here, I believe, for the way in which we will appraise *active holiness*, in the world in which we are.

In the Gospel there is a commandment which seems to me absolute, to disengage in order to engage ourselves in a new way: we are called to be 'in the world' and not 'of the world'. Not to be of the world is a radical disengagement. To be in the world is a total engagement, which has the same radical sense of totality as the Incarnation, which made of the Word of God, of the eternal Word, a human Name and a Presence of God in the flesh for ever. And there is that Gospel about rejecting those who are closest to us at the same time as there is the Gospel call to love the entire world with complete love, with sacrificial charity, totally engaged. In this there is, if not a paradox, at least a tension that often seems irreducible to certainties. The fact is that it is only to the extent to which we are disengaged that we can engage ourselves in a fruitful way. You know that if someone is drowning, you must jump in to rescue him but not let yourself be grabbed, because otherwise you both will drown . . . and you will get a posthumous medal for heroism, but that is useless. This is exactly the image of the Incarnation of the Son of God and of the incarnate way in which we must act in the world. We must *be in the world* without letting ourselves be caught hold of, we must be free of its grip. In terms of the theology of the Incarnation, this is called 'without sin'. In terms of our life it would be an exaggeration to say so even in the sense of an intention or a hope. But one must be sufficiently disengaged not to be an integral part of the sin of the world, even if we do not succeed in freeing ourselves entirely from this imprisonment. We are called to disengage ourselves from the bonds which hold us prisoners, in order to give ourselves freely as Christ did: 'Nobody is taking my life from me, I give it freely.' Thus we shall be able to live and die, but in Christ's way, in the way of a Christian: to die freely and not by suffocation. Christ became fully man but *without sin*. He lived our life and He died our death, without, however, participating in the evil which limits our life and provokes our death. As for ourselves, we must be *in the world* and not *of the world*. It is only under those conditions that we become capable of loving, not with a passionate love that imprisons us and imprisons others, but with a love that is free with the freedom of the children of God and that gives freedom.

In this *disengagement-engagement* there are two points to be raised. First, the necessity of disengaging from oneself, getting free from oneself. We have an exaggerated tendency to think that we are prisoners of other people. In reality we are prisoners of ourselves, for if we could only release ourselves from the grip of our ego, other people would have no power over us. They have power over us only by reason of our covetous desires and our fears and dreads. In this liberation from oneself there are several points which I would like to make you understand through images.

An English author whom I like very much and who has taught me a great deal, Charles Williams, in a book entitled: *All-Hallows Eve*, gives two images which, I think, are very illuminating. The story takes place in the city of London. A young woman has been killed in an accident. . . She is dead, but her soul still remains unmoving at the place on the bridge where death overtook her. . . She is dead, but her soul is not yet engaged in the

invisible world nor disengaged from the visible world, because
there is nothing in the invisible world that is familiar to her and
to which she could attach herself. She is still engaged in the
visible world because it is the only one which she knows. And
nevertheless we see her standing there surrounded by a world of
dead forms. She sees around her the banks of the Thames and
the houses which line them. Sometimes they are dead blocks with
black windows. . . sometimes those windows are lighted. But she
sees nothing besides this, because in the course of her whole life
she has never loved anything but herself. She is not connected
with any of the objects around her by the values of eternity,
values that can survive the death of the body. She perceives the
bridge on which her spiritual feet are weighing, and she sees as
cadaveric effects everything around her: nothing has life, for
nothing is joined to life either within her or outside her, as far as
she is concerned. . . At a certain moment something happens:
her husband crosses the bridge and she sees him. He is the only
person that she has ever loved—with an unstable love that had
no great depth, was often possessive and selfish—but this is
nevertheless a reality of fondness and love outside herself. From
the moment she perceives him a whole set of relations awakens
in her: through this fondness, this love that she has for her
husband she begins to rediscover things, human names which
suddenly acquire significance in eternity, places, situations. . . I
shall not tell you the story. What is important is to understand
that the perspicacity of this soul detached from the body and no
longer able to be connected to visible things through the body
and not yet linked to invisible things through an interior light,
this clearsightedness of the soul is awakened only at the moment
when love unites it to someone or something.

Here we have a beginning of liberation from the self: the
moment we become capable of loving we begin to disengage
ourselves from this prison which we are in relation to our person.
There is in fact a complete connection between 'loving' and
'dying'. To love means to disengage little by little from the
exclusive interest that one has in oneself and to transfer that
interest and that concern to someone. The deeper our love is and
the more all-embracing it is and the more it is disengaged from

the large categories of lust and fear, the more it frees itself from that aspect which C. S. Lewis so well describes as a diabolic love that consists in the wish to devour and assimilate the loved one, making of him a total prisoner. Ultimately, the more this happens, and the more the egoistic self gets free, the more free we are. Subjectively speaking, perfect love corresponds to death, that is, to a disappearance of our self-assertion, our affirmation of ourself by contrasts and opposition in terms of aggression and rejection. And the woman of Charles Williams' novel makes her first discovery: it is only to the extent to which we become capable of loving that we become capable of seeing and perceiving. To *see and perceive*, whether it be God or the world around us, whether it be the individual neighbour or the more or less complex situations that include our neighbours, all this is possible only insofar as we love them and accept dying in order to be able to see, live and participate.

There is a second passage in the same novel by Charles Williams that permits me to take up another aspect of these matters. We are surrounded by opacity, density: the world is not transparent to our gaze—and when I speak of the world I do not refer only to the cosmic world that surrounds us and that we may sometimes grasp in the light of God, because it does not present a danger to us: we can consider it in its natural beauty and its harmony, that is created or structured by man, without fear of being devoured or destroyed ourselves. But when we go back to our neighbour, whether in his individual aspect or in a wider collectivity as a social group, a society, he becomes more and more opaque because all the judgements that we pass, all the reactions that we have are defined by a 'How?': How does this person, this group affect *my* security, *my* integrity? To what extent is it a danger or a possibility for expansion? When it is a possibility for expansion it is almost always in a very mitigated, and especially Christianly mitigated, form, of an aggression. We make progress with our neighbour, in our group. We feel secure because we have increasingly put our hand on something. Or we ask: To what extent are we secure because the group is not attacking us? So we have a collection of opacities surrounding us. How are we to get through these opacities?

In the story by Charles Williams we find a further passage in which this girl, who is called Lester is beside the Thames. She sees it with her disincarnate eyes for the first time! For the first time she has no repulsion towards the sight of this Thames. Previously when she had looked at the river's edge she had always had a feeling of disgust: those thick lead-coloured, greasy, heavy waters, which transport all the city's refuse, had been repulsive to her because, having a body, she could only see them insofar as she imagined or thought of being able to drink them or jump in! But now Lester is free of her body: she has no body, she is a soul; so she has no fear of contact with those repulsive waters and as soon as she no longer fears contact, these waters no longer repel her. As the author says, she sees them as a 'fact', but as a fact which in itself has complete harmony. It is a harmonious fact because these oily, thick waters that are carrying all the city's refuse are exactly what the waters of this great river that goes through this big city should be. They correspond exactly to their own nature and their vocation. The moment she sees them as a legitimate fact which she can consider outside herself, she begins to discern what she had never seen before. Through this initial opacity she begins to distinguish a series of brighter and brighter patches of light. The deeper her gaze goes, passing through a greater opacity in order to reach a lesser opacity, the more she becomes aware that farther and farther away, closer to the bottom of the river, there is a light. And in fact, after first passing through opacities that diminish and then clear places that increase, at the heart of this river she succeeds in recognising, with the eyes that death has given her, the primordial waters, the waters as God created them in the first chapter of Genesis. And more deeply still, giving them their brightness and revealing their ultimate vocation, that water of which Christ spoke to the Samaritan woman.

This process is exactly the reverse of what often happens to us. We go from clarity to opacity. A first meeting can reveal a person to us in the light. And then with the bad clairvoyance, or rather the progressive blindness given us by selfishness, coldness, calculation, the fact that we think of everything in terms of ourself, we begin to discern greater and greater opacities. It is

only by an act of faith that we manage to say: 'Yes! this is a child
of light!' We say it, but very often we do not see it. And this is
why it is so often almost impossible for us—and when I say
'almost' it is a polite exaggeration—it is almost impossible for us
to see the face of Christ in the faces round about us. This is
important because it is fashionable now to look for God in one's
neighbour; it is not a new fashion: the desert saints of the third
and fourth centuries told us: 'If you have seen your neighbour,
you have seen your God.' But they saw him, whereas we most
often only say it! The fact is that in order to see the features
of Christ on our neighbour's face, which is sometimes very
difficult to read, we have to have in us the vision of Christ so as
to be able to project it on them. Then we see, in the light of
those divine features, that even in this portrait that sometimes has
become so hideous, we can recapture the features of *His image*.
I am not referring to momentary uglinesses, superficial evil, but
to a profound evil more important than what one does, the evil
that corrodes and causes the doer to lose the sense of the good—
and the sense of what is luminous in himself—such people as
one finds in prisons, everywhere, even in the Churches.

And so, at this moment, it is absolutely necessary to be able
to recognise the light places through the opacities and to recognise
in the features of the portrait, retouched from generation to
generation by the whole heredity of man, the conformity that
we have with God, His image. It is a question of recognising,
beyond the heavy materiality which leaps to our eyes, that which
transcends it. The world around us, including our neighbour, to
the extent that we lack this clairvoyance, this insight into the
depth, appears to us as an opaque mass. This mass, these volumes
that surround us, which we collide with and almost never meet—
for meeting somone is looking at him face to face, in depth—
these opaque masses belong to a material world to which we
implicitly deny depth. The material world has thickness: it has
no interiority. I think I am not being too complicated, in saying
that if you are in the presence of a glass sphere and you try to
penetrate it with your gaze, the farthest you can reach is its
centre: it is the ultimate point which cannot be transcended,
there is no other depth beyond. If you go further, you come out

again to the farthest surface. But all objects, even our neighbour, have only one density, one thickness, one heavy presence if we do not discover something more, that which is revealed concerning them by Holy Scripture, in which the psalm tells us: 'The heart of man is deep.' It is not a matter of the heart of flesh nor of a measurable depth, it is a matter of infinity, that is to say, of the fact that the heart of man cannot be measured, for it opens into the depths of God.

This is why, in all our inquiries into prayer, it is an interiority that we must seek, not the interiority of the psychologists, of a depth psychology that belongs to the realm of the created and at a certain point permits us to touch bottom, like the final and ultimate point that is the centre of a sphere. No, the depth we are concerned with is correlative with the fact that we are a will of God become tangible and visible. At the heart of our reality is the creative word of God. And the Word is the divine reality onto which we open in the depth. There is no use in looking for God round about. If we have not found Him within us, we shall never recognise Him in our neighbour, in historical events, in the heights.

If we have made the discovery of our neighbour in this way, if we have discovered that we have a depth that opens upon God, then we shall discover that very often our relationship with our neighbour can only be realised in silence. We all know in our everyday life those indescribable instants when at the most unexpected moment silence and peace descend upon us. When we are two who perceive this silence, when it envelops and lays hold of both of us, the words die on our lips and every gesture becomes a breaking of a relationship more important than anything one could express. If we let this silence penetrate us more and more deeply, there comes a moment when we can no longer express anything, when we feel that we are more and more close to a depth that we would never have known how to reach without the gift of God. When this silence has reached maturity, we shall discover that at the bottom of the silence there is a security and certainty that make us able to begin to speak. And then the words are sober: we search for them carefully before offering them; we utter them in a way that will not break this silence given by God.

There must always be, between us and God, a depth that we can reach—and I insist on this fact—that we should be able to reach. We should learn by the practice of the presence of God, by stopping time, by letting our being go deeper, to reach it almost at will, for it is our vocation to remain in the presence of the Lord. We should learn how to descend into ourselves when we are in the presence of our neighbour, whoever he is—not the pious one, the easy one, of whom we are ready to write in large letters: 'This is an image of God!' but the difficult neighbour, the unacceptable neighbour, the one who is an insult to all that we think of God and His Incarnation—we can then meet that neighbour in the place which no means of communication would enable us to reach, because we refrain from communicating on the level of words, gestures, external relations: we are not up to that, we are too small, too weak and friable for that.

If we take on our neighbour in this way, if we accept him in silence, we are making an initial act of essential importance: it is the act of justice—not an act of social justice, which is distributive, egalitarian—but a dangerous act of justice which consists, in the first place, of accepting our neighbour just as he is and giving him the right to be as he is, even if his way means our death and our destruction. It is an act of radical justice such as we see in God, who accepted fallen man instead of rejecting and destroying him; who accepted man in his downfall, knowing that the downfall of man meant the crucifixion of the Son of God. That is the act of Christian justice; it is there that justice begins, and not when we distribute the spiritual or material wealth equally or selectively. It is the moment when we allow the other person to be himself, whatever the consequences. It is only at this price that we can look and see in the features of the other person a living and glorifying projection of the face of the Lord.

This implies something I have already spoken of: *solidarity*, such as we see in Christ. This solidarity within fallen man, man in his final agony, in his radical godlessness, or rather his relative godlessness—for only Christ's is radical—this enables us to take up our responsibility. But here I must point out that Christian responsibility and solidarity have a quality that makes them inacceptable and impossible on a certain level, because they embrace both parties in conflict. A Christian can, in fact, support one human group against another, but he cannot undo his solidarity with the other in favour of the first. In a conflict, whether it be armed, social, economic or psychological, the Christian should be present at the point of rupture and accept in a total way the responsibility for both sides.

I shall first give you an example in terms of common law, from Church history. St Basil established a canonical rule which has never been applied—like so many canonical rules—which says that in case of armed conflict the Christian is called upon to take part in it, 'because' it says, 'if he had been a Christian worthy of the name, he would have been able to convert those around him to mutual love, and there would have been no armed conflict. But as it is he who bears the responsibility for the bloodshed, he should take part in this conflict. However, all the time the conflict is going on and for three years afterwards he must be excommunicated.' Here is a situation that is clear, precise, perfectly tenable theologically and of very great interest, which has never been applied because it implies at the same time the radical sense of bipolar solidarity and responsibility which is essentially identical to the Incarnation.

This is very important and I should like to say a few words about it. Remember the passage from the Book of Job I mentioned earlier. Towards the end of the ninth chapter Job in his despair turns to the empty, silent, cruel heaven and says: 'Where is the man who will stand between me and my Judge and put his hand on the shoulder of each of us?' Where is the one who will make an act of intercession?—for to intercede does not mean: to remind the Lord of what He has forgotten, as we so often do: 'Lord, this man is hungry, this one is thirsty; there is the war in Vietnam, tensions in America; there is this and that, do what is necessary?' No, intercession does not consist in simply telling God what He has forgotten to do and leaving Him in charge of the situation. According to the Latin word, to intercede means to take a step which brings us to the heart of a situation of tension, violence or conflict, and to stay there once and for all. What Job had sensed is that in this contestation between him and God, the only one who could place himself between the two would be someone who was the equal of each of the two, who could put his hand on the shoulder of the living God without sacrilege and on the shoulder of the man, in his agony, without destroying him. Here is a first vision of that which Christ will be, true God and true man, fully God and fully man, the One in whom and by whom the plenitude of Divinity has lived in the flesh, in our midst. And this act of Intercession by Christ which is the Incarnation—is a definitive act. Christ has not become man for a time: the Word of God is incarnated for all time.

This is what intercession is: at one and the same time an act which precedes prayer, a complete engagement which makes us simultaneously engaged and disengaged from the two sides, in solidarity with one side as well as with the other and, because of this, rejected by one as well as by the other. The Incarnate Word was killed by men because He was God; He was consigned to the cross because He was a man. He died a borrowed death which is a man's death. He was not accepted, because His witness was one that favoured God, from whom the people of Israel had already turned away. 'We want to be like all the nations!' they had said to Samuel when they asked for a king, and God answered Samuel: 'It is not you, it is I Whom they have rejected!' And the final rejection comes in these words of the people before Pilate: 'We have no other king than Caesar!'

The act of intercession is a prayer that is itself an act, and an act that is a prayer. Thus the action appears to us as a lived faith, something in which prayer becomes life. And if prayer and life are not the two faces of one same reality, one coin, neither one has authenticity.

Amos said that a prophet is one with whom God shares His thoughts and who not only receives the thoughts of God but, like a true prophet, proclaims them, lives them, witnesses to them, becomes an act of God. And it is to this that we are called in the Church, to be an act of God in the midst of the world. This is the special activity of the Church, which means that in all domains, political, social, economic, educative, the Christian's role has a peculiarity that makes it different from all the other functions in the world: it is an act of God and as such it can be in harmony with everything that goes on. One of the Christian obligations is precisely that of being not only the leaven in the dough but also the sword that divides the darkness from the light, truth from error, death from life, God from Satan, of being the stumbling-block, the scandal, the constant provocation, the constant affirmation that we are not seeking the kingdom of the Beast, that we do not accept a harmony based on apostasy, that we do not want a justice that is a denial of divine justice, a truth that is a refusal of the personal truth: 'I am the Truth!' and so on.

We are called to be that divine act by which God reveals Himself to the world, and, as such, our destiny can only be that of Christ. Yes, Christ did say to us: 'You will do greater works than mine. . .' and it is true: in His power and that of the Spirit we are called to complete a work in which His action was decisive but not final.

We must be a witness to the world of the Presence, of the transcendence, of the fact that the Eternal has become immanent and is in our midst: God is in us and through us, God Who has no common measure with man, the divine mystery. At the same time this God reveals Himself in an incredible way which man could not invent, in Christ, who appears to us defenseless, vulnerable, abandoned to the discordant wills of men, surrounded by hate, rejected, Who dies because of this and whose victory is in His humiliation.

I believe that what I have said can be referred back to the image that Chist gave us when he said: 'I consecrate myself, I sacrifice myself for them.' I don't know which of the terms should be used, because the Greek word is too rich to be translated by only one of them. It concerns a prime act of consecration: it belongs to God without limitations. *It is God*, and not only that but in its very humanity it has only one will, a life with God, and this in a free act in which the two wills find themselves united in a perfect way, in which the two natures are inseparable, in which the Word of God listens in on the will of God and watches in the depth what the Father is doing, then continues to act and work in the world, to accomplish now what the Father wills in the mystery of divine thought.

He sacrifices Himself. To sacrifice oneself now means to shed

one's blood or to impose limitations on oneself in favour of someone—this is the way we are always sacrificing ourselves, doing a
very little bit for our neighbour—but 'to sacrifice oneself' means
'to make oneself sacred, to consecrate oneself', and also to offer
oneself or be given in sacrifice. Did not Christ say: 'Nobody is
taking my life, I give it.' He gives himself up, He dies.

What is our attitude in such a situation? Is it not this combina-
tion of successive and disordered images that I have tried to give
you in the course of these talks? Is it not these images which
should permit us to feel our way, in the oneness of the ever contemporaneous Presence of God, into the multiplicity of ways in
which this total Presence brings itself to bear, expresses itself,
integrates itself into the variety of situations? But then our role
also consists in being perfectly obedient, not in the sense of
mechanical obedience, which would mean hearing orders and
carrying them out, but in the sense of an obedience in depth
which wants to listen in with vigilance, tension, alert vitality, in
order to hear and express what it perceives.

And this can be harmonious with what the world is seeking,
because the holy Spirit is not at work solely in the Church but
everywhere, with a power and a force that are sometimes impres-
sive. It is God who judges the Church at this moment by all that
goes on around it, by the persecution, by the protestation, by the
atheism, by the rejection of the caricature of God which we offer
for man's worship. And we most certainly must learn to assume
our responsibility for the sins of the past, and not to bewail ourselves as we recognise them but to see in them the judgement of
God as we endeavour to realise that which is the eternal truth
of God in the present situation.

I cannot give you recipes, I can only indicate *three elements*
as a conclusion to these considerations.

Interior contemplation, which is not a form of life but a
position vis-à-vis God, a standing before Him in a deepened
silence; the double and reciprocal presence of God with man and
man with God.

Prayer, in its active, human aspect, in its tension towards God,
with the resulting inward state of orientation towards God and
being present to God, and, lastly, its final state which is a position

in the world where we are: the prayer of the world to God, the articulation of the cry of the entire world to the living God. And this is obviously an ascetic exercise to the extent to which we are under our human vocation.

Finally, there is *action*, but as I said before, this action must be an act of God, by our instrumentality. Let us first learn to listen, hear, see and understand God, the world and our neighbour. And then to act not solely according to human wisdom but, above all, primarily on the basis of the divine wisdom which is revealed to us in Scripture, in life and in the sacraments—for the early Church strongly emphasised that these form the gateway to the knowledge of God and to action in the name of God. And if in all honesty we try to live in God and to live His presence in the world, I trust that in every situation God will teach us how to do His will: the ways may be different, opposed, incompatible. . . For if you read the Old or New Testament, you will see that there are no rules, no precepts—still less, recipes. There are divine responses which are mutually contradictory, because when God confronts this fragment of time that asks Him a question, He faces each situation with the whole of Eternity.

CHAPTER FIVE

JOHN THE BAPTIST

JOHN THE BAPTIST was the forerunner of Christ. He was the one who came before Him to make the pathway smooth, to make the crooked way straight. I believe this is exactly what all of us are called to do now with regard to other people, to make it smooth for them to find their way, and to help them to find a way which is straight, to the Lord.

I would like to single out a certain number of features in the person of St John the Baptist which I feel could teach us something about our situation, and what we should do, and what disposition of mind we should be in.

First of all, when you open St Mark's Gospel you find that he is defined as a voice that shouts in the wilderness. He is not even defined as a prophet or a messenger of God. He has got so identified with the message, he has become so one with God's own word which he has got to proclaim and to bring to people that one can no longer see him behind the message, hear the tune of his voice behind the thundering witness of God's own spirit speaking through him.

This is one thing which we should learn. Too often when we bring a message, people can perceive us and a message which perhaps comes through us, because we are not sufficiently identified with what we have got to say. In order to be identified we must so read the Gospel, make it so much ourselves, and ourselves so much the Gospel, that when we speak from within it, in its name, it should be simply—whatever words we use and I am not speaking of quotations—it should be simply the Gospel that speaks and we should be like a voice—God's voice. The second thing is that to attain to that state in which he could speak and not be noticed, in which all that people could perceive of him was a man who had been completely transformed into a message, into a vision, into a proclamation, meant he was a man who accepted to lay aside all that was selfish, grasping, all that was delighting selfishly in whatever he wanted to have. He had a pure heart, a clear mind, an unwavering will, a trained body, a complete mastery of self, so that when the message came, fear would not defeat him and make him silent; promises would not beguile him and make him silent, or simply the heaviness of the flesh, the heaviness of the mind, the heaviness of the heart, should not overcome the lightness and the lightening power of the spirit. This is something that is also our task.

I do not speak now of the forms of asceticism or the way in which one does it, but we must learn to be free, and to be free, we must acquire mastery over ourselves. This is terribly important, and to achieve that, we must learn to look and learn, but not only to look at people and situations—look at God and learn and hear. Obedience is vital. To obey the will of God requires a training. The will of God is madness, the will of God is paradoxical. You cannot adhere to the will of God for good reasons. More often what He often asks is an act of folly which we would not otherwise dare to commit. Remember Abraham: God promised him a son, and the son was born. He promised that the son would be a beginning of a generation of people more numerous than the sands of the shores; and Abraham believed Him. And then God commanded him to take his son and to bring him, a blood offering, to Him, and Abraham did it. He did not tell Him. 'That contradicts your previous injunction; this is contrary to your promise.' He trusted the Lord and did what the Lord said at that moment, leaving the Lord to fulfil his promises the way He knows.

This happens to us also. We are called to act day after day, moment after moment, according to the will of God revealed within that moment when the difference between Christian action and just action resides in the fact that action must be planned, action must not contradict action. There are no returns and moves back and sideways; it must be a straight course. If we want to act within the will of God, we must be like Christ who listens and proclaims the word, who gazes attentively at God who is at work, and when he has seen, performs the action which is implied in the willing, in the thinking, in the rich creative imaginings of God. This we must learn, but to do this, we must learn to master ourselves and become capable of acting not only when we agree, not only when we understand, but when we disagree somewhere within the old Adam in us, or when we cannot understand but say 'I trust you, I will act with folly.'

The forerunner has another quality. Remember what he said: 'I must decrease in order that you should increase.' Our role is to cut straightways; our role is to make rough ways smooth, but when we have done this, we must step aside, and allow the Lord of life, Him for whom we are preparing the way, to come in a lordly manner, or with the humility of Christ come with the simplicity of His entry into Jerusalem. And we must be forgotten because as long as we loom large, people will not see Christ.

There is a way in which our absence is as necessary to the glory and action of God as our presence is at another moment.

Remember the other way in which the forerunner is defined. When speaking about himself he says that he is the friend of the bridegroom—the one who so loves the bride and the bridegroom that he brings them together, so loves them that he is the protector of their love, of their intimacy, of their peace, of their meeting, and whose vocation is to bring together bride and bridegroom— the living God and the living soul, and then stand guard to pro- tect this meeting against any intrusion, but not to be party in this meeting, to be outside; that is his particular form of love and service. At the same time, we must be prepared also to face, in the name of the bride and groom whom we serve, in the name of this mystery of love, the coming of the kingdom; the conquest by God of all that is death, evil, sin, separation, meanness which is to small for the measure and the stature of man. We must be prepared to speak to man the truth, God's own truth, not our own.

Remember the way in which the forerunner spoke to Herod, the way in which he spoke to the multitudes. To do this we must have authority, and authority is not gained either by rank or by social standing. Authority is gained by this fusion between our

own will and God's own will; our own word and God's own
word, our own life and God's own life, us and Him; then we
can speak, and then our words, however hard, however sharp,
however truthful, however deep they will go down, however
much they separate body and soul, our words then will also be
words of love, because God's word is always the word that gives
truth and light, love and life. And then we must be prepared
not to see the results of what we have done. The forerunner died
before he had seen Christ; coming to the end of his mission and
fulfilling the promises of his vocation, he died. He died of his
message, he died of the truth of God, he died because he had
become identified with the message and the truth, because he
was a friend of the bridegroom that had to decrease so that the
bridegroom should have all the field.

We must be prepared for that. In every case, with regard to
every soul, to every group, to every event, to every situation,
there is this time for the forerunner and there is the time for him
to decrease and die out—perhaps not physically, but in the
memory of people, in their hearts, in their relationships. We must
be prepared never to be remembered because what has been sown
by the word is so rich, so overwhelming, that the forerunner, the
one that has prepared the way, the one that has ploughed, the one
that has sown, can be forgotten. This is joy. It is joy to see Christ,
the Lord, grow to his full stature, to occupy his real position, to be
the king and the lord and master, and the brother and the saviour
and the joy and the freedom of those to whom we have come
and said 'He is coming, open yourself to him.' This is what the
scriptures call repentence or conversion.

Now I will tell you what a priest at the end of a Roman Mass
says to the people—'Go'—it is a dismissal; but what is a
dismissal? Does it simply say the service is over, out of the chapel,
while the congregation in a rather ambiguous way says: 'Thanks
be to God.'

No, it is not that. The dismissal means this: You have been
on the Mount of Transfiguration, you have seen the glory of
God, you have been on the road to Damascus, you have faced
the living God, you have been in the upper chamber, you have

been here and there in Galilee and Judaea, all the mysterious places where one meets God, and now having spent several days with him, he says now that so much has been given—go, your joy will never abandon you. What you have acquired, you will never lose as long as you remain faithful. Go now, and if truly you have discovered joy, how can you not give joy to others? If truly you have come nearer to truth, how can you keep it for yourself? If truly something has been kindled in you which is life, are you going to allow anyone not to have a spark of this life? It does not mean go round and tell everyone specifically religious things or use clerical phrases. It means that you should go into the world which is yours with a radiance, with a joy, with an intensity that will make everyone look at you and say 'He has something he hadn't before. Is it that truly God has come near? He has something he never had before and which I do not possess— joy, life, certainty, a new courage, a new daring a vision, where can I get it?'

People will also say to you, 'Mad you are'. I answer in those cases, and they are many, I say 'I am mad, but one thing I find strange. You who are wise call to the mad man, and the mad man is happy, alive and you feel dead; let us share my folly, it is God's folly.'

You are now going to start. With God you go now, with him on all the ways, on all the roads; you can dance on the Mount of Transfiguration, you can bring concreteness of life for others. May God bless you in it with joy. I don't know any other words than 'with joy'—go with joy, bring joy, and then you will have brought everything else, because God is joy, he is life, he is intensity.

And may God bless you, and not only you but everyone, your family, you friends, those who have been, those who have not been here, those whom you will meet throughout your lives— bring them a spark.